सद

Sadācāraḥ

SADACHAARAH

by

Ādi Shankaracharya

Commentary by

Swamiṇi Vimalananda

Central Chinmaya Mission Trust

First Edition September 2005 - 3000 copies
Reprint June 2008 to September 2011 - 2000 copies
Reprint August 2014 - 1000 copies

Published by:
Chinmaya Prakashan
The Publications Division of
Central Chinmaya Mission Trust
Sandeepany Sadhanalaya
Saki Vihar Road, Mumbai 400072, India
Tel.: +91-22-2857 2367, 2857 5806
Fax: +91-22-2857 3065
Email: ccmtpublications@chinmayamission.com
Website: www.chinmayamission.com

Distribution Centre in USA:
Chinmaya Mission West
Publications Division
560 Bridgetown Pike
Langhorne, PA 19053, USA
Tel.: 1-888-CMW-READ, (215) 396-0390 Fax: (215) 396-9710
Email: publications@chinmayamission.org
Website: www.chinmayapublications.org

Printed by:
SAGAR UNLIMITED
Unit No. 1, Y.A.C. Indl. Estate,
Kondivita, Andheri (E), Mumbai - 400 059
Tel: 28362777 / 30829777
Website: www.systemsprinters.com

Price: Rs. 90=00

ISBN: 978-81-7597-330-5

Acknowledgement and Dedication

Yathā dṛṣṭi tathā sṛṣṭi—As the vision, so the world appears to us. Ādi Śankarācārya sees everything with a Vedantic vision. In *Aparokṣānubhūti* (verses 104-124), he envisages the various steps of *Rāja Yoga* (*yama, niyama* etc.) as Vedantic meditations. In *Sadācāra* he does the same with our daily spiritual practices and activities like bathing, eating etc. This really caught my imagination.

Pujya Gurudev and Pujya Guruji have always been the inspiring force that gives wings to my imagination and allows me to fly high through my writings.

This time Ganesh did ground me for a while, but finally managed to type out the hand-written manuscript and see the book to completion before himself flying off on his own to join the Vedanta Course in Mumbai. *Au revoir* and blessings to him.

Smt. Radhika Krishnakumar makes it easy for me to make mistakes as she is so good in editing them. This makes my flying safe.

First impressions are important. The attractive cover page designed by Shri Krishnamurthy of

Mayapuri Graphics, Chennai helps the reader's mind to take off on the journey with me. My grateful pranams to all.

We are grateful to Shri T. B. Thakur, President, Chinmaya Mission Tarapur, who is sponsoring the first edition of this book. He has always been a generous donor and an active sevak in the Mission. May Pujya Gurudev's blessings be on him and his family.

Vedanta is the joy of my life and writing my thrill. Thank God for the joys and thrills of life that keep me focussed on Him.

This is a humble offering to Pujya Guruji on his birthday. All credit for the thoughts expressed go to the Guru Parampara. All shortcomings are due to my limitations.

Swamini Vimalananda

7th September 2005

Śaṅkaraṁ Śaṅkarācāryam

A brief life-story of Ādi Śaṅkarācārya (adapted from 'Sankara–The Missionary', a Chinmaya Mission Publication).

The greatest of realised Masters, a devout devotee, an ideal *karma yogi,* unsurpassed in *haṭha yoga,* a world teacher, a perfect organiser, a far-sighted statesman, a *Yuga Purusha,* an exemplary man of letters, a deeply compassionate down-to-earth soul, the very incarnate of Lord Shiva—such descriptions are just a few surface waves that describe the infinite and bottomless ocean of virtues that is Bhagavan Adi Shankaracharya.

Birth

Shankara was born to Shivaguru and Aryamba at his maternal home, Veliyanad, Kerala (The Chinmaya Mission runs a research centre, Chinmaya International Foundation, at the same site. An *akhaṇḍa dīpa* [a lamp that is kept continuously lit] burns in the room where he was born).

An interesting anecdote describes his divine birth. After having waited long for a child, his parents prayed to Lord Shiva at Thrissur, Kerala. The Lord appeared and asked whether they desired to have a brilliant boy who would have a short life span, or an ordinary son who would live long. They chose the former and within a year Aryamba gave birth to a child. The parents named them Shankara, being the gift, nay, the very incarnation of Lord Shankara.

Childhood and Education

He was initiated into the study of the alphabets (*akṣara abhyāsa*) at the age of three and soon could read and understand entire books. His father died when he was three. His mother performed his thread ceremony (*upanayanam*) and sent him to a residential school (*gurukula*) when he was five. He learnt all that his teacher knew in three years and compiled a book when he was just six years of age. Once when he was seeking alms (*bhiksha*) he was moved by the abject poverty and yet intense devotion of the lady serving him and he spontaneously composed and sang the famous *Kanakadhārā Stotram*. To her utter amazement, the Goddess of Wealth (*Lakshmi*) showered golden fruits before her, forever removing her poverty.

Once, grieved by the strain his mother had to oblation to bathe and wash her clothes at a river far from her home, he prayed to the Lord for help. The next morning, wonder of wonders, the river Purna was flowing gently by the side of his house!

Sannyāsa

Despite his desire, his mother did not grant permission to the eight year old Shankaracharya to adopt the holy order of a renunciate. Once while he was bathing in the river, a crocodile caught his leg. As he was being dragged down, he asked his mother's permission to become a renunciate. In her helpless and horrified state, she granted him permission. With the Sun-God as a witness, Shankaracharya said, "*Sannyasto'ham*—I have renounced" thrice. To everyone's surprise, the crocodile released him, and he walked out of the jaws of death, untouched. After assuring his mother that he would be with her at the time of her death, he left home to become a wandering monk, at the tender age of eight years.

Meeting his Guru

In a cave on the banks of river Narmada, at the pilgrimage centre of Omkarnath, lived the great Master Govindapadacharya. When Shankaracharya reached his great Master, he was in meditation. With eyes closed, he asked, "Who are you?" His impromptu famous composition *Daśa ślokī* poured out. "I am neither the earth, nor water... but the one changeless Shiva." The Master accepted him as his disciple and in three years, he had mastered all that was to be learnt.

Once when his master was in deep meditation, there was a flood in the mighty river and the water was about to enter the cave. The disciples were in a dilemma. Shankaracharya placed his begging bowl (*kamaṇḍalu*) at the mouth of the cave, and on touching it, the waters receded much to the wonder and relief of all.

To test his knowledge, the Master asked him to write a commentary on the *Viśnu Sahasranāma* (The thousand names of Lord Vishnu). His brilliant commentary convinced the Master that his disciple was more than capable of writing commentaries for great works like the *Upanishads, Brahmasutras, Geeta* and endless other compositions. The Master left his mortal coil, and Shankaracharya moved on to Banaras, from where he travelled to Badri, Kedarnath and Uttarkashi, all the time engaged in writing and teaching.

The Missionary

Once Bhagvan Veda Vyasa came as an old *brāhmin* to test Shankaracharya's knowledge and command over the Scriptures. After days of scholarly discussions, Veda Vyasa revealed his true identity and complemented Shankaracharya. His ordained lifespan was only sixteen years, which was soon to end. Veda Vyasa blessed him with sixteen more years to propogate his great spiritual knowledge. Shankaracharya blessed the great *Pūrva Mīmāṁsā* scholar—Kumārila Bhatta, with a *mantra* so that he could die peacefully as he was burning alive on a funeral pyre. He had a scholarly discussion and defeated Shri Mandana Mishra (who later became one of his four main disciples—Shri Sureshwaracharya) and his wife Ubhayabharati(who was the incarnation of Saraswati, the Goddess of Knowledge).

Shankaracharya fearlessly offered his head to be sacrificed by a *kapalika* for a *tantrik* ritual. His disciple Padmapadacharya invoked Lord Narasimha, who killed the Kapalika.

When he heard of his mother's serious condition, Shankaracharya, with his *yogic* power, travelled by air and reached her side. He composed and sang the *Shiva Bhujangam* and *Vishnu Bhujangam* and immmediately the attendants of Shiva and Vishnu appeared to take her on her onward journey. Shankaracharya, a *sannyasi,* being the sole survivor, wished to do the final rites of his mother. The traditionalists were shocked. How could a renunciate do so? They refused to help him. Shankaracharya carried her body himself, and lit the pyre alone by just chanting some *mantras.* On seeing such power, those who had gathered were repentant.

Dig-vijayam Tours—Conquering the Directions

In those days of slow transport and rough terrain, Shankaracharya, along with his disciples and hundreds of devotees travelled from Kanyakumari in the South to Afghanistan and Kashmir in the North; and from Assam in the East to Gujarat in the West. He was met by kings and scholars, seekers and devotees, the traditional thinkers and the modern. He taught them and guided them. He formulated the *Pañcāyatana Pūjā* to resolve differences in the worship of various deities. He consecrated many temples including the famous Badrinath temple, Kamakshi temple at Kanchi, Jagannath temple at Puri etc. He renovated many others. He ascended the *Sarvajña Pīṭha* in Kashmir with great respect from all after having vanquished all the known scholars of his time in discussions. He composed various hymns like *Soundarya Lahari*, as he visited different temples. Once his *Param Guru* (Guru's Guru), Gauḍapādācārya visited him and blessed him.

Last days:

Shankarcharya, with his few main disciples, went to Kedarnath. He solved all their doubts and prepared them for his final departure. He entrusted the work of continuing his work through four main disciples by establishing four *muṭhs* in the North,

South, East and West. Thereafter he chanted the *Daśa Ślokī,* which he had composed on meeting his *Guru,* absorbed his mind in meditation and dissolved his body by *yogic* power.

His disciples came down to the plains to carry on the task given by their *Guru.* Padmapadacharya established the Govardhan Mutt at Puri in the East. Hastamalakacharya established the Kalika Mutt at Dwarka in the West. Sureshwaracharya established the Sharada Mutt in Sringeri in the South, and Totakacharya established the Jyotir Mutt at Badri in the North.

Shankaracharya's compositions are innumerable and of the highest brilliance. It would be impossible to fully recount his incomparable and invaluable contribution to the renaissance of the Hindu Dharma. It is impossible to enumerate all the works and glories of this great Master.

Only a special divine person, a *Yuga Purusha,* could have accomplished so much in so short a time. He was indeed the Lord Shiva incarnate—*Śaṅkaraṁ Śaṅkarācāryam.*

INTRODUCTION

An action by itself is inert. Consciousness or the Self enlivens it and emotions and thoughts propel it. They together give action the potency to produce results.

Consciousness of course naturally and choicelessly enlivens every thought and action as awareness is Its very nature. The sun does not consciously shine or activate & energise human beings on earth. It does so by its very nature. Emotions and thoughts however consciously prompt and propel actions by giving them power and direction just as the driver guides the speed and direction the vehicle takes.

We call actions thoughtless, indifferent, half-hearted, distracted, mechanical, well-planned, focussed, kind, cruel etc. depending on the emotions and thoughts behind them. The *namaskāra* of an air-hostess is often called mechanical, the hand-shake of a diplomat formal, the promises of a politician false, etc. Such actions lack the right emotions and thought behind them They are therefore devoid of essence (*asāra*). We call the smile of a child genuine, the words of a saint touching or the master piece of an artist inspired, for these actions have in them the essence (*sāra*) of truth, goodness or appropriateness. (*Sad bhāve sādhu bhāve ca—Sad/Sat* implies truth/goodness—*Geeta*). Such actions or conduct (*ācāra*) backed by the right emotions and thoughts is called *Sadācāra*.

Pujya Guruji Swami Tejomayananda once said, "If our actions are not according to our values, then gradually our values fall to suit our actions." All of us value rising early (though our definition of 'early' may differ!). One who for some weeks rises an hour later than he originally intended to, slowly finds that the time that he valued earlier as ideal for waking up has also fallen by half an hour if not an hour. A value falls with every compromise with it. On the other hand if we are uncompromising in our actions, they then improve to suit our values. For instance, selfish and demeaning acts like match-fixing drop when a cricket team plays solely for the glory of the country. *Sadācāra* is to put this 'value add' to all our actions.

The *Dharma Shastras* (scriptures on right living) guide us how to add value into our mundane daily actions through a meaningful daily plan (*dina caryā*) and inspiring life plan (*jīvan caryā*). They teach us *Sadācāra*. Adi Shankaracharya goes one step further. He teaches us how to make our daily routine and life, not just meaningful and inspiring, but a means to reach the Supreme. That according to him is *Sadācāra.* Also all actions of those who have reached the Supreme (*sat*) are *Sadācāra*.

The least that is expected of man is to be humane. Then alone can he claim to be a human being. "One who is ever engaged in good deeds, is cultured, follows his duties acccording to his stage and status in life and behaves well, is alone called a human being."

Nityānuṣṭāna-nirataḥ sarva-saṁskāra-saṁskṛtaḥ
Varṇāśramā-sadācāra-sampanno nara ucyate.

Sadācāra is meant to make us 'humane'-beings.

The qualities of *tamas* (inertia, evil etc.) and *rajas* (selfishness, agitation etc.) are obstacles to material or spiritual success. They should be overcome by cultivating *sattva guṇa* (alertness, selflessness etc.). *Sattva guṇa* thereafter is sublimated with the Knowledge of the Supreme, to reach a state beyond all qualities (*guṇātīta*). (*Tamodvābhyām rajas sattvam, sattvam śuddhena naśyati—Vivekachudamani*)

Adi Shankaracharya urges man from being ordinary and doing uninspired actions to first become good and do meaningful and inspired actions. Thereafter *sadācāra* shows him the path of becoming extraordinary and divine.

As the vision, so the world appears to us. In this text, Adi Shankaracharya teaches us how to look upon the world and all actions with a Vedantic or non-dual (*advaitic*) vision.

* * *

No effort is successful without the blessing of the Lord and therefore all spiritual texts commence with an invocation prayer (*maṅgalācaraṇa*).

सच्चिदानन्दकन्दाय जगदङ्कुरहेतवे ।
सदोदिताय पूर्णाय नमोऽनन्ताय विष्णवे ॥ १ ॥

saccidānandakandāya jagadaṅkurahetave|
sadoditāya pūrṇāya namo'nantāya viṣṇave|| 1||

1. नमः=Salutations; विष्णवे=to Lord Vishnu; सत्-चित्-आनन्द-कन्दाय=of the nature of Existence-Consciousness-Bliss; जगत्-अङ्कुर हेतवे=the Cause of the world; सदा-उदिताय=the ever-present; पूर्णाय=the complete; अनन्ताय=the eternal.

1. Salutations to Lord Vishnu of the nature of Existence-Eonsciousness-Bliss, the cause of the world, the ever-present, the complete and the eternal.

Once Lord Vishnu started worshipping Lord Shiva* with a thousand names, offering a lotus with

---

* Though many stories in Hindu religious literature refer to many gods, it is desirable to keep in mind that they are all various manifestations of one god-principle alone.

each name chanted. To His dismay He found that He had only 999 lotuses. If He got up midway, His worship would be considered incomplete. He finally removed one of His eyes and offered It, considering It as a lotus (since devotees call Him *Kamalanayana*—One who is lotus-eyed). Lord Shiva was pleased with His worship and appeared before Him to bestow on Him complete fulfillment of worship.

All actions, done by even the great, by their very nature are finite and imperfect. It is the Lord's blessings alone that compensates for the imperfections and gives glory to all we do. Hence the invocation prayer.

The verse serves as an auspicious (*maṅgala*) beginning to the text. Prayer or prostration to the formless Truth cannot be done remaining different from It. When such a prayer is attempted, it becomes meditation. Hence we meditate on the Truth as an auspicious beginning to the text. The same infinite Truth manifests as *Iśvara,* the Lord of the Universe, addressed here as Vishnu. Our prostrations to Him.

* * *

After the invocation prayer the author states the *anubandha catuṣṭaya* –

सर्ववेदान्तसिद्धान्तैर्ग्रथितं निर्मलं शिवम् ।
सदाचारं प्रवक्ष्यामि योगिनां ज्ञानसिद्धये ॥ २ ॥

sarvavedāntasiddhāntairgrathitaṁ nirmalaṁ śivam|
sadācāraṁ pravakṣyāmi yogināṁ jñānasiddhaye|| 2||

2. प्रवक्ष्यामि=I shall explain; सदाचारम्=*Sadācāra*; निर्मलम्=which is pure; शिवम्=auspicious; ग्रथितम्=expounded; सर्व-वेदान्त-सिद्धान्तैः=by all the Vedantic texts; ज्ञानसिद्धये=for attainment of Knowledge; योगिनाम्=of the *Yogins*.

2. *I shall explain Sadācāra, which is pure, auspicious, and expounded by all the Vedantic texts for the attainment of the Knowledge of the Yogins.*

The *anubandha catuṣṭaya* are:

1. *Adhikārī*: The qualified person for the study of the text: A fifth grader would not pick up a book of pure science meant for a post graduate student, even for a casual look. For whom is *Sadācāra* meant? It is not meant for a *bhogī*—one whose mind is only involved in pleasure and indulgence. *Sadācāra* helps those who are seeking something higher, nobler and more exalted in life (*yogīnām*).

2. *Viṣaya*: The theme of the text: The *Vedas* are the very basis of our philosophy, religion and way of life

(*Vedo'khilo dharma-mūlam*). They essentially cover the topic of *Dharma* (how to live well in this world) and *Brahma* (how to realise the Supreme Truth behind the creation). The former which includes good spiritual conduct (*sadācāra*) is required to realise the latter (which is also called Vedanta). Hence the text talks of good spiritual conduct which is both purifying (*nirmalam*) and sanctifying (*śivam*).

3. *Prayojana*: The purpose served: Even a fool does not act without a purpose (*prayojanam anudiśya mando'pi na pravartate*). Gain is always in terms of knowledge. Only when I 'know' I have money am I able to enjoy and spend it. If it were not known, it would be as good as not having it. Here too the purpose is to gain knowledge (*jñāna siddhaye*) of the Supreme Truth, as that alone would give me supreme happiness.

4. *Saṁbandha*: The relationship between the theme and the purpose: By study and reflection on the text, and following the good spiritual conduct indicated (*viśaya*), the spiritually inclined seeker (*adhikārī*), gains the knoweldge of the Truth which is the very purpose served (*prayojana*).

It is easier to emulate the conduct of others than to translate their words into our conduct. In fact most of our values are not taught but caught from people we idolise or those around us. The *Geeta* too says that the conduct of the great becomes the hallmark for others to emulate.

What then is the role of the good advice of great men and scriptures in our life? They do provide a guide and ideal which we must internalise and follow. Is knowing more important than doing? It is knowledge alone that backs all actions and therefore knowing is the first step in doing. However only well-assimilated knowledge manifests as conduct and not half-assimilated knowledge. Every smoker knows that cigarette smoking is injurious to health, yet his knowledge does not percolate into action as it is not internalised enough.

However, the process of changing our actions to match our values often seems difficult and therefore the wise advice the reverse. By consistent good conduct, our knowledge and values change, become well-grounded and consequently choicelessly practised as good habits. Eg. by bathing daily (even if forced at times) right through childhood, we developed the value for cleanliness, which now as adults has become second nature to us.

The *Manu Smṛti* says, "By good conduct one gains a long life, good progeny, lasting wealth and it puts an end to all weaknesses, faults and vices.

Ācārāllabhate āyuḥ ācārādiptitāḥ prajāḥ
Ācārād-dhanam akṣayyam ācāro hantyalakṣaṇam.

The following twelve practices in our daily routine (*dina caryā*) constitute right conduct (*sadācāra*) and should be followed by all desiring freedom from sorrow—the remembrance of the Lord in the morning, cleansing of the body, bathing, expiatory acts to remove sins, prayers, repetition of the name of the Lord, offering water to one's ancestors, offering oblations to the fire, worship of the Lord, observance of silence, meditation and appropriate eating.

Prātaḥ smaraṇaṁ śaucaṁ casnānaṁ cāghamarṣaṇam
sandhyā japas-tarpaṇaṁ ca agnihotraṁ tathā-arcanam.
Maunaṁ dhyānaṁ bhojanaṁ ca sadācāraḥ prakīrtitāḥ
mumukṣuṇāṁ to kartavyāḥ svātmanārthe to jñāninām.

From verse 3-15, Adi Shankaracharya shows us how each of the above practices of our daily life can be converted into meditation on the Supreme.

The twelve practices of *sadācāra* are being explained at three levels:

1. As a regular practice that all of us should undertake as explained by the *Dharma Shastras* through which we attain outer prosperity (*abhyudaya*) and inner unfoldment (*niḥśreyasa*).
2. As an exercise in meditation for the seeker of Truth.
3. As the natural state of a realised person.

* * *

The following verses speak of what one should do on waking up in the morning.

प्रातः स्मरामि देवस्य सवितुर्भर्ग आत्मनः ।
वरेण्यं तद्धियो यो नश्चिदानन्दे प्रचोदयात् ॥ ३ ॥

prātaḥ smarāmi devasya saviturbharga ātmanaḥ|
vareṇyaṁ taddhiyo yo naścidānande pracodayāt|| 3||

3. स्मरामि = I remember (contemplate); प्रातः = at dawn; यः = that; भर्गः = effulgence; देवस्य सवितुः आत्मनः = of the Self-resplendent Sun; तत् वरेण्यम् = that most excellent one; प्रचोदयात् = may inspire; नः = our; धियः = intellects; चित्-आनन्दे = towards Consciousness-Bliss.

3. *I remember (contemplate) at dawn, that effulgence of the Self (which is comparable to the effulgence) of the resplendent Sun. May that most excellent one inspire our intellects towards (the Self which is of the nature of) Consciousness and Bliss.*

Many machines, gadgets and appliances that we buy these days come with an instruction manual and a guaranteee card. The salesman assures us that the machine will outlive the guarantee period if used according to the instructions given. Malfunction, or breakdown is caused due to abuse or misuse. The human body and mind is the best made machine in the creation. It is guaranteed to live for a hundred years in a healthy condition if used according to the norms of right living as given in the Scriptures.

Elders therefore bless us with the words, "May you live for a hundred years (*śatāyuṣī bhava*)." Most of us are ignorant of these rules or choose to ignore them and pay a heavy price mentally and physically. Why would a heart which is in fact guaranteed for 200 years fail and collapse at the age of 35 years, but for its abuse!

***Prātar utthānam*: Getting up in the morning:** Like most other beings, man's natural body cycle coincides with the 24 hour day-night cycle of nature. Man like many other living beings is meant to awaken early refreshed and revitalized by 6 - 8 hours of sleep at night. In the present day most of us disrupt this natural body cycle by keeping awake till late and sleeping in late. A lot of our mental stress and physical ailments are caused or aggravated due to this. The first instruction of the Scriptures is to awaken early. This is possible only if we sleep early. It is often heard, "Early to bed, early to rise, makes a man healthy, wealthy and wise." Ayurveda says, "One who rises early becomes beautiful like a lotus, gains fame, intelligence, wealth, health and long life."

Varṇa kīrtiṁ matiṁ lakṣmīṁ svasthyaṁ-āyuśca vindati

Brāhme muhūrte saṁjāgrac-chriyaṁ vā pañkajaṁ yathā.

(Āyurveda: Bhā sāra: 63)

The *Manu Smṛti* says, "*Brāhme muhūrte utthāya...*" wake up at *Brahma muhūrta*. The night is divided into four quarters (*prahara*). 6 – 9 pm, 9 – 12 midnight, 12 – 3 am and 3 – 6 am. The first quarter is meant for dinner and *sāttvik* entertainment; the second and third quarters are meant for sleep and one is expected to wake up between 4 and 6 am, i.e. before the sun rises (*prātaḥ kāla*). At that time nature is at its best, the air is rejuvenating, the body refreshed and the mind relatively free from worldly agitations and pre-occupations. Everyone of us resolves to reform first thing in the morning and regret the wrong we have done the day before, as in a pure mind, what is right and wrong is clearly perceived.

***Prātaḥ smaraṇam*: Early morning remembrance:** One cannot be hypocritical first thing in the morning and so the thoughts and words one generally speaks as soon as one gets up reflects one's character. Shri Hanuman recognised Vibhishana as a great devotee when he woke up chanting the name of Lord Rama. It is common experience to wake up with the thoughts we have slept with. If we wish to start the day with good thoughts, it would be a good idea to sleep with such thoughts. It is said, "*...dharma-arthaṁ cānucintayet.*"—"On waking up, one must entertain elevating thoughts, think of God, meditate on the Truth, remember what you have to do and plan out the day ahead." It is one of the best times for students to study, for creative and subtle thinking, problem solving, planning etc. One must start by remembering who we are in essence: "I remember the pure Self within, who is Existence-Consciousness-Bliss... and not this body made up of five elements."

(*Prātaḥ smarāmi hṛdisaṁ sphuradātmatattvam ... na ca bhūtasaṅghaḥ*—Śaṅkarācārya)

Thereafter we remember the Lord, the creator of the Universe: "I remember the Lord Shiva, who bears the Ganges on His head ... who is the herb that cures us of the disease of *saṁsāra*."

(*Prātaḥ smarāmi gaṅgādharaṁ ... saṁsāra-roga-haram-auṣadham-advitīyam*)

We remember the great people who belonged to our culture and tradition: "I salute the great king Nala, Yudhishthira ... the holy cities of Ayodhya, Mathura ... the great women—Ahilya, Draupadi ... "

(*Puṇyaśloka nalo rājā ... ayodhyā mathurā ... ahilyā draupadī ...*)

We recollect the virtues we wish to imbibe during the day: "... (I remember) Bhagirath and his fortitude and hard work..."

(*... Bhagīrathaṁ dhīram ugra-yatnam ...*)

***Kara darśanam*: Looking at one's hands:** Once we remember the Lord we are supposed to see the palms of our hands held together. The Geeta says, "Lift yourself by yourself." It is our own effort that brings success. One who awaits the turn of fate, waits forever. Hands symbolise self-effort (*puruṣārtha*). We see our hands and pray, "Wealth (*Lakṣmī*), Knowledge (*Sarasvatī*) and the Lord (*Govinda*) reside in my hands (May I attain these through self-effort today)."

Karāgre vasate lakṣmī karamūle sarasvatī
Karamadhye tu govindaḥ prabhāte kara-darśanam.

***Pṛthvī sparśanam*: Touching the Earth:** As one rises from the bed one respectfully touches the earth in obeisance saying, "I postrate to You, Mother Earth, bedecked by the mountains and oceans, the wife of Lord Vishnu. Do forgive me for trodding on You."

Samudra-vasane devī parvata-stanamaṇḍale
Viṣṇu-patnī namastubhyaṁ pāda-sparśaṁ
kṣamasva me.

The five elements are the very support of life in us. The earth has matchless beauty and symbolises fortitude and forgiveness. In Indian culture, it is considered disrespectful to touch anything worshipful with our feet. We therefore apologise to the Motherly Nourisher for stepping on Her and prostrate to Her in gratitude. How then can we exploit that what we worship each day?

***Śubha darśanam*: Seeing auspicious objects:** What we see and hear influences what we think. We therefore pray, "May I always hear and see auspicious sounds and sights..." (*Bhadraṁ karṇebhiḥ śruṇuyāma devāḥ, bhadraṁ paśyema-akṣabhir yajatrāḥ...*). It is good to wake up to the sounds of prayers, chantings, chirping of the birds, seeing the photographs of the Lord, one's Guru, saints, the sunrise, nature etc. They have a refreshing soothing and elevating effect on the mind. The Scriptures say, "Difficulties vanish when one sees a wise man, a happily married woman, a cow, sacred fire/a lamp, and a worshipper—when one gets up in the morning."

Śrotriyaṁ subhagāṁ gāśca agniṁ agnicitam tathā
Prātarutthāya yaḥ paśyet āpadbhyaḥ sa vimucyate.

Till now we viewed waking up as a part of our daily routine, now let us see the verse from the Vedantic stand point. It indicates meditation on one of the most famous and efficacious *mantras* of the *Vedas*—the *Gayatri Mantra*. It is called *Gayatri* as one is protected from harm by its very chanting (*gāyantaṁ trāyate*). Rishi Vishwamitra discovered this most famous *mantra* of the *gāyatrī chanda* (metre) through which *Savitā*—the Sun God is worshipped. This *mantra* is used as a prayer (*prārṭhanā*), for repetition (*japa*), as part of regular worship (*pūjā*), in the fire ritual (*homa*) or for meditation (*dhyāna*). Its simple meaning is "We meditate on the resplendent Sun, may it inspire our intellect." The Sun can be revered and worshipped from three stand-points.

1. ***Adhibhautika***: The *mantra* refers to the Sun that gives light, energy and nourishment to all life on earth. It is the focal point around which our solar system revolves. It symbolises selfless service, inexhaustible energy, brilliance, punctuality etc. We meditate and pray to that symbol of light.

2. ***Adhidaivika***: The Sun is the presiding deity of the intellect. The intellect is the driver of this body (*buddhiṁ to sārathiṁ viddhi*). We meditate and pray to *Sūrya devatā* to make our intellect brillliant, inspired and drive us forward along the path of goodness and success.

3. ***Ādhyātmika***: The Sun is the principle of Consciousness because of which all thoughts and actions are possible. It alone manifests as life in us. We meditate on the pure Self (*ātmā*) the resplendent light (*vareṇyaṁ bhargaḥ*) of Consciousness Bliss (*cidānanda*). May our intellects be inspired to dwell, reside and be one with It. Adi Shankaracharya obviously refers to the *ādhyātmika* stand-point in this verse.

***Vareṇyaṁ bhargaḥ*: The resplendent light:** The Self is the very principle of knowledge, awareness or illumination because of which any knowledge as thoughts or illumination as light is possible. In the light of the Self alone does the Sun shine. It is independent, ever present, homogenous, does not wax or wane and is self-evident. It is therefore the best (*vareṇyam*). Being the very life in us, it is most auspicious and sacred. It is our own true nature. It is me, myself. This is the meditaion that one should practise each morning before sunrise (*prātaḥ kāla*).

* * *

The morning meditation continues–

अन्वयव्यतिरेकाभ्यां जाग्रत्स्वप्नसुषुप्तिषु ।
यदेकं केवलं ज्ञानं तदेवास्मि परं बृहत् ॥ ४ ॥

anvayavyatirekābhyāṁ jāgratsvapnasuṣuptiṣu |
yadekaṁ kevalaṁ jñānaṁ tadevāsmi paraṁ bṛhat || 4 ||

4. अस्मि = I am; एव = verily; तत् = that; परम् = supreme; बृहत् = Infinite; यत् = which; केवलम् = homogenous; एकम् = one; ज्ञानम् = Knowledge; अन्वय-व्यतिरेकाभ्याम् = which is established by the logic of invariable concomittance; जाग्रत्-स्वप्न-सुषुप्तिषु = with regard to the waking, dream and deep-sleep states.

4. *I am verily that supreme, infinite, homogenous one Knowledge, which is established by the logic of invariable concomittance with regard to the waking, dream and deep-sleep states.*

The method of *anvaya-vyatireka* is used in Vedanta to prove the presence or the cause of a thing. *Anu+aya = anvaya*—meaning that which is continuous or goes everywhere i.e. is ever-present. *Vi+ati+rikta = vyatirikta = vyatireka*—meaning that which is specially and completely empty i.e. totally absent.

The three states of waking, dream and deep-sleep that each of us goes through daily are mutually absent (*vyatireka*) in each other. For instance there is no trace of my dream riches or of my peaceful sound sleep in my agitated and poverty-stricken waking state. We cannot carry anything physically to the other state. The experiences of one state are totally negated in the other two states.

Howeever, I, the pure Self, the illuminator of the three states am always present (*anvaya*). I am aware of the waking experiences, the dream world and the absence of the two in the deep-sleep state. I am the one (*ekam*) pure Consciousness (*jñānam*) that witnesses the presence and absence of the three states. If the illuminator of the three states was not the same, how could we have known the presence or absence of shift from one state to another. For example, if a different person read each page of a book, how could he or she find a link between the pages or understand its content?

***Kevalam*: One alone:** Differences are categorised as –

i. within one species (*sajātīya*): each human being is different from the other.

ii. between species (*vijātīya*): the human being is different from a monkey though he/she may at times act like one!

iii. within a thing (*svagata*): my hands are different in name, form, position and function from my feet.

The Self, being one, non-dual and partless, is without any differences.

***Param bṛhat*: The Supreme Big:** The Self is bigger than the biggest, i.e. formless, substanceless, all-pervading and infinite.

One must meditate, "I am the one, alone, infinite, Consciousness that is the witness of the three states—waking, dream and deep sleep."

* * *

If I am the non-dual Consciousness, then why do I perceive the world as something different from me? Is there not the duality of the perceiver and the perceived?

ज्ञानाज्ञानविलासोऽयं ज्ञानाज्ञाने च पश्यति ।
ज्ञानाज्ञाने परित्यज्य ज्ञानमेवावशिष्यते ॥ ५ ॥

jñānājñānavilāso'yaṁ jñānājñāne ca paśyati|
jñānājñāne parityajya jñānamevāvaśiṣyate|| 5||

5. अयम् = This; ज्ञान-अज्ञान-विलासः = is the play of knowledge and ignorance; च = and; पश्यति = is seen; ज्ञान-अज्ञाने = in knowledge and ignorance; परित्यज्य = after having renounced; ज्ञान-अज्ञाने = both knowledge and ignorance; ज्ञानम् = Knowledge; एव = alone; अवशिष्यते = remains.

5. *This is the play of knowledge and ignorance and is seen only in knowledge and ignorance. After having renounced both knowledge and ignorance, Knowledge alone remains.*

***Jñāna-ajñāna vilāso'yam*: This (creation) is a play of knowledge and ignorance:**

a) The entire world is made up of inert and changing matter. Its very existence and functions depends on the principle of Consciousness (*jñāna*). The combination of the two inert (*ajñāna*) and Consciousness (*jñāna*) is not possible like the co-existence of light and darkness. Yet the entire world is perceived as the play of inert matter existing in the light of Consciousness.

b) Consciousness is one without a second. Its power of creation is called *maya*. In the presence of Consciousness, *maya* creates this world with its two powers. The veiling power (*āvaraṇa śakti*) veils Consciousness due to which we remain ignorant of it (*agrahaṇam* or *ajñāna*). Thereafter the power of projection (*vikṣepa śakti*) superimposes what is not there due to which we experience this world as real (*anyathā grahaṇam* or *jñāna*). For instance, The rope is veiled to my vision and the snake is projected and seems real. This world is therefore the play of the two powers of *maya*.

c) The world is experienced as pair of opposites. Were it not for sorrow, heat, dishonour etc., we would never comprehend joy, cold, honour etc. Knowledge (*jñāna*) and ignorance (*ajñāna*) represent all pairs of opposites, as this world is largely a play of the pairs of opposites.

d) In the waking and dream state I experience "I am so-and-so" and the world as "I know this or that" (*jñāna*). The deep sleep is experienced as "I do not know anything, the world or myself" (*ajñāna*). This entire creation is the play of these three states (waking, dream and deep sleep) whether of the individual (*jīva*) or the Totality (*Īśvara*).

***Jñāna-ajñāne parityajya jñānam eva avaśiṣyate*: When the knowledge-ignorance is removed, Knowledge alone remains:** The perception and play of knowledge-ignorance lasts till we inquire into the truth behind it (*vicāra abhāva jīvana*)—"Who am I?" "What is the changeless truth behind this changing world?" "Is what I perceive alone real?" Such questions remove the false notion we hold regarding ourselves and the world and lead us to our own true nature which alone is the changeless Truth behind this world. The play of *maya* (*yā mā sā māyā*—that which is not but appears to be is *maya*) ends and Consciousness which is me, alone remains. I am the substratum, the Reality behind *maya*, that is, behind all names and forms, all pairs of opposites and duality as it is perceived. They are all illusion though they are perceived and have no power to affect me. When we imagine a grinning ghost on a lamp post, we are paralysed with fear. On seeing the post, the illusion of the ghost ends. Once we have seen the post, when the shadow effect once again shows us a ghost-like image, we only enjoy the play of light and shade, knowing fully that the post alone exists.

* * *

Cleanliness is next to godliness. After remembering Him we get into the act of clearing all the waste collected and becoming clean (*śauca*).

अत्यन्तमलिनो देहो देही चात्यन्तनिर्मलः ।
असङ्गोऽहमिति ज्ञात्वा शौचमेतत्प्रचक्षते ॥ ६ ॥

atyantamalino deho dehī cātyantanirmalaḥ ।
asaṅgo'hamiti jñātvā śaucametatpracakṣate ।। 6 ।।

6. देहः = Body; अत्यन्त-मलिनः = is extremely impure; च = and; देही = the owner of the body; अत्यन्त-निर्मलः = is extremely pure; इति = thus; ज्ञात्वा = after having known; अहम् = I am; असङ्गः = unattached; एतत् = this; प्रचक्षते = is declared; शौचम् = as *Śoucam* (Purification).

6. *The body is extremely impure and the owner of the body is extremely pure. This state of knowledge that "I am unattached" is declared as* Śoucam *(Purification).*

***Śoucam*: Cleanliness:** Each day we dispose the garbage from the house, dust, sweep and swab it etc. These tedious daily tasks even if boringto perform, are important to make our living comfortable. The body similarly produces waste which needs to be cleared each morning. In fact, the body regularly brings out dirt from the eyes, ears, nose, throat, skin, anus etc. as sweat, phlegm, urine, stools, gases etc.

Even though what is taken in is air, water and food, what is brought out is foul-smelling waste and dirt. We need to clear this waste and clean the body in order to keep it healthy and comfortable to live in. The Scriptures like a mother raising her child, gives us guidelines as to how to keep ourselves clean after passing urine and stools (*śaucācāra*).

***Dantadhāvana*: Cleaning one's teeth:** Even presently in rural India and previously all over the country, people cleaned their teeth by chewing a branch of certain trees. Thereby not only were their teeth cleaned and flossed, but the gums and teeth also were strengthened, the voice became sweeter (*vadaryāṁ madhuraḥ svaraḥ*), the speech clearer (*udumbare vāksiddhiḥ*), memory improved (*apamārge smṛtir-medhā*) bad breath removed (*nimbsca tilake śreṣṭha*) and the herbal juice had an antiseptic effect in the mouth. Realising this many tooth pastes are now available in the market with extracts of liquorice, lime, neem etc. The process ended by cleaning the tongue and washing the mouth and eyes with cool water (*prakṣālaten-mukhaṁ netre svasthaṁ śitodakena vā*).

There is even a prayer addressed to the twig/toothbrush to bestow long life, strength, fame, a glow, progeny, cattle, wealth, knowledge of the Truth and a good memory.

Āyur-balaṁ yaśo varcaḥ prajāṁ paś-vasūni ca.
Brahmaprajñāṁ ca medhāṁ ca tvaṁ no dehi vanaspate.

To the extent one practices these clean habits, to that extent does one develop dispassion towards one's own body and towards others also (*śaucāt sva-aṅga-jugupsā paraiḥ asaṁsargaḥ—Patañjalī Yoga Sūtra*).

The crystal, though colourless, when put over a red cloth, looks red. The body is ever impure, is born, grows, decays and dies. Its impurities are specially repulsive when the body is diseased or when it emits pus, vomit, blood etc. The pure Self within, out of ignorance has identified with this body and suffers due to it (*saṁsāra doṣa*). To remove the impurity of ignorance and cleanse oneself of the false identification with the body is Vedāntic *śauca*. To realise the pure Self is the final or ultimate act of purification. It need not even be repeated daily as the Self is eternally pure.

***Atyanta-nirmalaḥ*: Totally pure:** Impurity is something other than a thing. For example, when dust particles fall in water, we call it dirt. When there is water alone, it is called pure water. The Self is one without a second. Anything other than it is an illusion and an illusion is insubstantial and cannot affect its substratum like the colour seen in the crystal. Hence the Self is totally pure.

A saint's looks were critisised by a stranger. He said, "What you say is true. This body as every other body is indeed censurable. It is the indweller, the Lord alone, who is worshipful."

Once Upasani Baba lived in a cage to teach his disciples a lesson. When asked the reason, he said, "You too are caged in your body with all its filth. You think you are this filthy body, but I remain as the pure Self within."

The *Chhandogya Upanishad* gives two apt similies to explain this point. The horse through a strong jerk of its body, shakes off all the dirt that hangs onto its mane. In Indian mythology, the bodiless demon Rāhū, is believed to swallow the moon causing an eclipse. The moon after a time frees itself from Rāhū's mouth to shine in its original glory. Ignorance born identification with the body is the 'original sin' which leads to many more. When this is shrugged off (like the dirt on the mane of the horse) the Self shines forth (like the moon released from Rāhū's mouth) in its pristine glory (*Aśva iva romāṇi vidhūya pāpaṁ, candra iva rāhor-mukhāt pramucya, dhūtvā śarīraṁ akṛtaṁ kṛtātmā brahmalokam abhisaṁbhavāmi*).

***Taila mardana*: Oil massage:** Many Indians, even today apply and massage warm oil on the body from head to toe, every day before a bath. The feet and head are given extra attention during the massage and a couple of drops of oil put in the ears as well. The oil massage is especially given till the child is a year old and then continued periodically. The oil used is of mustard/olive/sesame/coconut (depending on the weather of the place and many other factors) and mixed with herbs, flowers, natural perfumes etc.

Vāyu, the presiding deity of air is also the presiding deity of the skin, the sense organ of touch. We take in air, water and other nutrients not only through our nose and mouth, but also to some extent through our skin. We also remove waste in terms of gases and sweat through the skin. Hence the pores of the skin need to be kept clear and clean and the skin nourished and healthy. This is effectively achieved by an oil massage.

The foot massage benefits the eyes. The head massage nourishes the hair making them thicker, softer and longer. One of the reason for early greying and balding amongst Indians nowadays is due to the stopping of this pratice of massaging the head and hair with oil. The oil in the ear imporves hearing, and the gentle massaging of the ear lobes benefits the joints and several other organs of the body.

Of the five elements, the fire element taken into the body as butter, oil or clarified butter (*ghee*) gets divided into three parts. The gross part helps in bone-formation, the middle, to produce marrow and the subtle aspect influences our speech. Hence we talk of fiery speech and hot discussions. The oil taken in through massage is hence very beneficial for the formation and strengthening of our bones and to endow us with good speech. Interestingly, the great Charaka says that the oil taken in through a massage is much more beneficial than butter or ghee eaten. Besides specific benefits to individual parts, it prevents aging, adds a glow to the skin, improves circulation, nourishes the entire body, and gives us sound sleep. The Ayurvedic oil-massage treatment is known to do wonders for many diseases and ailments like spondylosis, arthritis etc.

* * *

One needs to bathe daily, once, twice or thrice; according to the climate one lives in. Let us see the *dhārmic* and Vedantic significance of a bath:

मन्मनो मीनवन्नित्यं क्रीडत्यानन्दवारिधौ ।
सुस्नातस्तेन पूतात्मा सम्यग्विज्ञानवारिणा ॥ ७ ॥

maṇmano mīnavannityaṁ krīḍatyānandavāridhau |
susnātastena pūtātmā samyagvijñānavāriṇā || 7 ||

7. मत्-मनः = My mind; मीनवत् = like a fish; नित्यम् = always; क्रीडति = sports; आनन्द-वारिधौ = in the ocean of Bliss; तेन = by that; सम्यक्-विज्ञान-वारिणा = by the

excellent waters of knowledge; सुस्नातः = one becomes well-bathed; पूतात्मा = and the Self is purified.

7. *My mind, like a fish, always sports in the ocean of Bliss. By those excellent waters of knowledge, one becomes well-bathed and the Self is purified.*

A cold shower or a hot bath in the morning, evening or night is most refreshing, improves our hunger, brightens our mood and reduces the tiredness and burdens of the day. With it one is ready to face the world once again.

It is believed that a bath in a holy river or lake washes away our sins. We therefore invoke the holy waters even in our bath tub, bucket or shower with the verse, "O Ganga, Yamuna, Godavari, Saraswati, Narmada, Sindhu and Kaveri, please come into this water."

Gaṅge ca yamune caiva godāvari sarasvati
Narmade sindhu kāveri jale'smin sannidhiṁ kuru

The very act of bathing can become the worship of the Lord if we consider that it is to the Lord within that we offer this bath (*snāna*) and special bath (*abhiṣeka*) with shampoos, bathing salts, perfumes etc., instead of the milk, honey, ghee (clarified butter) etc. that we generally offer to His idol!

The bath is basically an act of purification. The *Dharma Shastra* talks of seven types of bath:

1. ***Māntram*:** As an act of purification, during the dawn and dusk prayers (*sandhyā*), we chant certain prayers like "*āpohiṣṭā mayo bhuvaḥ...*" whilst touching various parts of our body. This is called a *mantra* bath (*āpohiṣṭādibhir-māntram*).

2. ***Bhaumam* or *Pārthivam*:** When mud is applied to the entire body, it is called 'mud bath' (*mṛdālambhaṁ ca pārthivam*). Mud packs are used in beauty parlours to enhance looks and in naturopathy clinics as a cure for many ailments.

3. ***Āgneyam*:** Purifying the body by applying the holy ash is called 'fire bath' since ashes are from the sacrificial fire (*āgneyaṁ bhasmanā snānam*). Great *Yogīs* are known to stay in the freezing Himalayan region with just the holy ash smeared all over the body.

4. ***Vayavyam*:** The cow is considered sacred by Hindus and the dust of the earth which the cow walks is applied as an 'air bath' (*vayavyaṁ gorajaṁ smṛtam*).

5. ***Divyam*:** Bathing in the rays of the sun is called a 'divine bath' (*yattu sātapa-varṣeṇa snānaṁ tad divyam ucyate*). The sun provides vitamin D and nourishes the body. Sun bathing is now popular all over the world. People apply sun-tan lotions and spend hours

in the sun. In ancient India people applied various oils on their skin and did the same.

6. *Varuṇam*: Bathing in a river, pond, lake, waterfall or well is called a 'water bath' (*vāruṇaṁ cāvagāhaṁ tu*). Nowadays we bathe in a bath-tub, with a bucket or under a shower, with special effects of a river, waterfall etc. achieved through a jacuzzi or shower jets! The *Yājñavalkya Smṛti* talks of the ten virtues gained by a bath as good looks, glow, strength, purity, long-life, health, non-covetousness, good sleep (without bad dreams), fame and memory.

Guṇā daśa snānaparasyā sādho rūpañca tejasca balaṁ ca śaucam

Āyuṣyam ārogyam alolupatvaṁ dusvapna-nāśaśca yaśaśca medhā.

The same becomes a complete purificatory bath when it includes mentioning the intent (*saṁkalpa*), chanting Vedic prayers (*sūkta-paṭhanam*), sprinkling water on oneself (*mārjanam*), the washing away of sins with specific prayers (*aghamarṣaṇam*) and offering oblations to the deities (*devatā tarpaṇam*).

Aghamarṣaṇam and *tarpaṇam* are dealt with separately in verse 8 and 11 in this text.

7. *Mānasam*: Meditation on the Self is called 'mental bath' (*mānasaṁ hyātma-cintanam*). It is the most enjoyable form of purification which Adi Shankaracharya too indicates in this verse.

When we bathe in a river, we do not just dip and come out unless it is too cold. We splash around, paddle, dive, swim and play around enjoying ourselves thoroughly. A fish is born and lives in water. Swimming is effortless and natural to it. It swims all its life tirelessly. It struggles for life if taken out of water. It thrives where there is plenty of water and food which too grows in water. It is always clean when in water and does not need a bath like a land animal or bird.

The mind which like the fish meditates on the Self within, remains ever pure and always revels in the infinite ocean of Bliss which is filled with the water of Self-knowledge. Whether it lies dormant in the deep-sleep state or plays around in the waking or dream world, the mind remains ever in Bliss. Even a seeker of Truth feels purified by the practice of meditation. Then what to speak of the realised one who is ever in meditation (*sahaja samādhi*)! King Janaka, when he first saw Shri Rama and Lakshmana, said, "My mind never wanders away from the Bliss of the Truth. The fact that my mind is pulled towards them (Rama and Lakshmana), proves that they must be Truth Incarnate alone."

The *Tulsi Ramayana* says, "The mind of the devotee always revels in the infinite glories of the Lord like the fish enjoying itself in plentiful water (*sukhī mīna jahāṁ nīra aghādhā...*).

The Ganges emerges from the matted locks of Lord Shiva. The Lord is the very source of this river of knowledge and devotion. Bathing in it purifies and fulfills us with knowledge, devotion and Bliss.

* * *

Within each of us there exists to a lesser or greater degree a sense of self-condemnation, guilt and regret over the small or big errors we have committed. This nagging feeling within us is an obstacle to both material and spiritual progress. The means to wash it is now explained.

अथाघमर्षणं कुर्यात् प्राणापाननिरोधतः ।
मनः पूर्णे समाधाय मग्नकुम्भो यथार्णवे ॥ ८ ॥

athāgh-amarṣaṇaṁ kuryāt prāṇāpāna-nirodhataḥ।
manaḥ pūrṇe samādhāya magna-kumbho yathārṇave।। *8*।।

8. अथ = Afterwards; कुर्यात् = one should accomplish; अघ-मर्षणम् = expiation; प्राण-अपान-निरोधतः = by the restraint of the inbreath and the outbreath; समाधाय = after having placed well; मनः = the mind; पूर्णे = in the Absolute; यथा = like; मग्नकुम्भः = a pot immersed; अर्णवे = in water.

8. *Afterwards one should accomplish the aghamarṣaṇam (expiation) by the restraint of the inbreath and the outbreath, after having placed*

well the mind in the Absolute, like a pot immersed in water.

Action is the insignia of life. Throughout our lives, we do physical and mental actions, some of them knowingly and some unknowingly, harmful to ourselves or others. Such actions, which result in sorrow are called sins (*pāpa*). They leave a negative impression within us like guilt, regret, self-condemnation, conflict, dislike etc. *Aghamarṣaṇa* (*agha* = sin + *marṣaṇa* = rub), the act of expiation is to consciously wash-off the ill-effects of the sin from our mind.

This is not a licence for us to act as we wish and later on through an action feel free of guilt. It is a means to become more aware of the wrong done knowingly or unknowingly, accept that it was wrong, become conscious of its ill-effects on the mind, feel deep sense of regret, repent sincerely and thereafter carry on with life with a new resolve and without the burden of guilt on our conscience. Also by *aghamarṣaṇam* we cannot cancel the result of wrong done by us. A person cannot get away with stealing and expect not to be caught or punished, just because he performed an act of expiation. But it would definitely prepare him to face the result in a more positive manner. (The Christians have the 'confession' where one tells the priest about the sin committed and takes on punishment as a means of purification).

Aghamarṣaṇam is a part of the daily *sandhyā* prayers done at dawn and dusk. Water is taken in the right palm, and air is exhaled through the right nostril into the water. The wrong done is recollected with repentence as we exhale. The water is then thrown away without looking towards the left. It symbolises, "I have washed off the negative feeling and shall not look back but instead start (not the sins!) anew."

The act of expiation frees us of the negative effects of sin (*pāpa*) but the realisation of the Self washes of the very ego that sins (*pāpī*). There is no more the chance of committing wrongdoings thereafter. How it is done is explained in this verse.

Prāṇāyāma consists of *pūraka* (to fill the lungs) or inhalation, *recaka* (to empty) or exhalation and *kumbhaka* (like in a pot) or retention. The air can be either inhaled and retained within (*antar kumbhaka*) or exhaled and the emptiness prolonged (*bāhya kumbhaka*). Through proper guidance and practise, the effort of the practioner is to increase the span of *kumbhaka*. The practise of *prāṇāyāma*, amongst its various benefits, purifies the mind and frees it of its negative tendencies and feelings. Hence it serves as an act of expiation.

However Adi Shankaracharya advocates that along with retaining the air within or without, the mind should be retained in the Self which like the air is both within and without. When the mind is thus stilled, there are no incoming or outgoing thoughts, no sin or regret, no sorrow or guilt, but the pure state of awareness.

A mud pot held in the ocean is filled with and pervaded by water. Every space within and every pore of the pot is permeated with water. Similarly the mind of the practioner becomes completely still and soaked in and by the Truth. Where is the place for sin or regret? All the past guilt is naturally washed off and there is also no scope for future guilt. Can the infinite Self do wrong or regret anything? Can the ego—the doer of all actions, which is washed off, be caught or punished?

* * *

At dawn and dusk the mind is naturally quiet. What should one do at such times?

लयविक्षेपयोः सन्धौ मनस्तत्र निरामिषम्।
स सन्धिः साधितो येन स मुक्तो नात्र संशयः ॥ ९॥

layavikṣepayoḥ sandhau manastatra nirāmiṣam|
sa sandhiḥ sādhito yena sa mukto nātra saṁśayaḥ|| 9||

9. सन्धौ = At the conjunction; लय-विक्षेपयोः = of the dissolution and projection; मनः = the mind; तत्र = there; निरामिषम् = is desireless; येन = by whom; सः = that; सन्धिः = conjunction; साधितः = is achieved; सः = such a person; मुक्तः = is liberated; अत्र = in this matter; न = there is no; संशयः = doubt.

> 9. *The mind is desireless at the conjunction of the dissolution and projection. The one who has achieved that conjunction is said to be liberated. In this matter, there is no doubt whatsoever.*

The power of prayer is well-known by those who pray regularly. The sages found the right time, place and ideal means for all our daily practices so that they become most efficacious. They therefore recommended that we pray every day at dawn, mid-day and dusk through a ritual called *sandhyāvandanam*. At these times the atmosphere is spiritually surcharged and so the mind easily quietens.

Sandhyā vandanam means 'salutations to the Lord'. *Sandhyā* literally means the meeting point or the conjunction of the day and night (*ahorātrasya sandhi*). The best time for the morning prayers is when the stars are still around (*prātaḥ sandhyā sanakṣatra*). The mid-day prayers should be done when the sun is overhead (*madhyāhno madhya-bhāskara*) and the evening prayers should be done as the sun is setting (*sasūryo paścimā sandhyā*). At such times we should not eat, sleep or while away our time in gossip or watching TV, but pray or do something contemplative (*na aśniyāt sandhivelāyām na gacchannāpi samviśet*).

Sandhyā is not a desire prompted action (*kāmya karma*) but a duty (*kartavya karma*) that contributes to our outer prosperity (*abhyūdaya*) and inner unfoldment (*niḥśreyasa*). Just as we bathe, eat and sleep daily, we should pray also. Even if we are busy or feel lazy, we should pray at least once every day.

The various steps of the *sandhyāvandanam* ritual are accompanied by appropriate *mantras*. The main steps are:

1. ***Ācamanam*:** Sipping water for purification of the body and mind.
2. ***Gaṇeśa dhyānam*:** Meditation on Lord Ganesha to ward off hindrances.
3. ***Prāṇāyāma*:** Purification of the vital airs.
4. ***Saṁkalpaḥ*:** Reciting the intention and purpose behind the ritual.
5. ***Mārjanam*:** Cleansing by sprinkling water on various parts of the body.
6. ***Prāśanam*:** Drinking water to remove undesirable attitudes and actions.

7. ***Ācamanam and Mārjanam*:** Repetition of steps 1 and 5.

8. ***Arghya-pradānam*:** Offering water to the Sun.

9. ***Aikya-anusandhānam*:** Contemplation on the identity of the individual and the Truth.

10. ***Deva tarpaṇam*:** Offering water to the nine planets (*navagrahas*) and twelve deities of the twelve months.

11. ***Japam*:** Starting with meditation on Lord Ganesha, *prāṇāyāma*, *saṁkalpa*, invoking Goddess Gayatri, establishing the power and essence of the Gayatri *mantra* in the hands and body (*nyāsa*), chanting the Gayatri *mantra* and bidding farewell to goddess Gayatri and Lord Surya (*upasthānam*).

12. ***Vandanam*:** Respectful prostrations to goddess Gayatri, the Deities of the directions (*dig-devatā*), Lord Death (*yama*), Lord Vishnu, and Lord Sun (*Sūrya-nārāyana*).

13. ***Samarpaṇam*:** Offering the entire ritual to the Lord.

The Vedantic way of observing *sandhyā* is now explained:

1. When the mind concentrates on the breathing or the repetition of the name of the Lord,

it reaches a state of absorption (*laya*) like a bird caught up in a net (*vāyu-rodhanāt līyate manaḥ jāla-pakṣivat rodhasādhanam—Upadeśa Sāra*). Once the concentration is lost, the mind goes back to its natural state of distraction (*vikṣepa*). The seeker should attempt to quieten the mind (make it free from distraction) and yet not go into a state of absorption, but hold it in a state of full awareness. To put it in the language of Shri J. Krishnamurti—'It is not a state of concentration or distraction, but a state of choiceless awareness'.

2. When we are asleep, the mind is dormant (*laya*) and when we are awake, it is full of thoughts (*vikṣepa*). Each morning and evening, we should practice *sandhyā* just as we awaken or fall asleep. In the morning, we should become fully aware of the moment when we are out of sleep but not yet awake to the world, and at night, of the moment when we have withdrawn from the world and are not yet asleep. By remaining still in this state, we realise our true nature of pure Awareness, free from all desires and thoughts.

3. The mind is a flow of thoughts. Pujya Gurudev Swami Chinmayananda in his own unique style advises us to "meditate on the point

where the last thought is already 'thoughted' and the next thought is not yet 'thoughting'"—the meeting point of two thoughts or the gap between them.

4. This meditation can be practised in many ways by observing the gap between two *mantras*, two sounds, two breaths etc.

This same concept is illustrated by the incarnation of Lord Shiva and Shri Krishna at midnight and of Lord Rama at noon. Hiranyakashipu, the demon, received the boon that he would not die by day or night, on the ground or in the air, by any weapons or natural forces, inside or outside nor by man or animal. The Lord incarnated as *Narasimha* (half-man half-lion) and killed Hiranyakashipu at dusk, holding him in his lap, at the threshold of his palace and ripping him open with his claws. The ego (Hiranyakashipu) is sustained by the concepts of time, place, objects etc. When these are removed, in that timeless, thoughtless state, the ego dies and the infinite Self manifests.

Man usually avoids voids. He fills his time, mind and home with activities, thoughts and things respectively. But if he pauses to look into the 'now and here', the gap between the activities and thoughts, he realises that infinite Self and becomes ever fulfilled.

A mythological story says that Brahma, the Creator, too got attached to his own daughter Sandhyā—one of his most beautiful creation.

In understanding, *Sandhyā* is a state of pure awareness. Desire cannot touch this state and defile it. The mind absorbed in it becomes desireless (*nirāmiṣam*).

* * *

Breathing is natural to man and he does so throughout his life. Is there a spiritual practise which can be done as effortlessly and continuously throughout our life? The verse explains.

सर्वत्र प्राणिनां देहे जपो भवति सर्वदा ।
हंस सोऽहमिति ज्ञात्वा सर्वबन्धैर्विमुच्यते ॥ १० ॥

sarvatra prāṇināṁ dehe japo bhavati sarvadā|
haṁsa so'hamiti jñātvā sarvabandhairvimucyate|| 10||

10. सर्वत्र देहे = In all bodies; प्राणिनाम् = of beings; सर्वदा = at all times; जपः = *japa*; भवति = happens. (अ)हम्-सः = I am That; सः अहम् = That I am; इति = thus; ज्ञात्वा = having known; विमुच्यते = one becomes liberated; सर्व-बन्धैः = from all bondages.

10. The japa: "I am That, That I am" happens at all times in all (bodies of) beings. Having known thus, one becomes liberated from all bondages.

With the right instruments and sufficient resources (*yantra*), the proper procedure and skill (*tantra*) and the mental application and knowledge (*mantra*), anything can be achieved. In fact, *'mantra'* has the power to produce or procure the *'yantra'* and activate both the *'tantra'* and *'yantra'*.

The repetition of one *mantra* is called *japa* (*mantraikasya āvartanaṁ vai japo vāk-karma hyucyate*). The *mantra* can be a letter like *bīja mantra—hrīṁ, klīṁ* etc., a Vedic *mantra* like the Gayatri *mantra*, Paurāṇic *mantra* like *'Om namo bhagavate vāsudevāya'* or just the name of the Lord like Rāma, Rāma... or Kṛṣna, Kṛṣna... The repetition of the Gayatri *mantra* is an important part of the ritualistic dawn and dusk prayer (*sandhyā*). *Japa* can thus be a part of a ritual or an indepenent spiritual practice. Using the beads (*japa mālā*) aids concentration and it can also be used for counting. Some use their hand (*kara mālā*) for the same.

There are three types of *japa*:

1. ***Vācika*** : Repeating the *mantra* aloud, with proper intonation, and clear pronunciation is known as 'verbal *japa*'.

Yad-ucya-nīca-svaritaiḥ śabdaiḥ spaṣṭa-padākṣaraiḥ.
Mantram-uccārayed-vācā vāciko'yaṁ japa smṛtaḥ.

This is easier and most commonly practised.

2. ***Upāṅśu*** : Repeating the *mantra* softly, with hardly any movement of the lips such that none other can hear is called 'silent *japa*'.

Śanair-ucyārayen-mantram-iṣad-auṣṭau na cālayet.
Aparair-na śrutaḥ kiñcit sa upāṅśur-japa smṛtaḥ.

This requires more concentration.

3. ***Mānasika*** : When the *mantra* is repeated mentally, it is called 'mental *japa*', also when each letter and word is contemplated upon.

Dhiyā-yad-akṣara-śreṇyāṁ varṇād-varṇa padāt-padam.
Śabdārtha cintanaṁ bhūpa kathayate mānaso japaḥ.

This is the most difficult and efficacious form of *japa* and is also a technique of meditation which can lead to a state of Realisation.

Japa protects us from the cycle of birth and death (*janmanā pāti*). It is the easiest spiritual practice and can be done by anyone at any time under any circumstances. Certain Vedic *mantras* have rules of chanting, but just the name of the Lord can be chanted or sung in any which way that suits the practitioner.

Japa makes the mind pure, subtle and concentrated. It is a practice ideally suited for modern times when the mind is so distracted that meditation is impossible and rituals too time-consuming and tedious. The name of the Lord (*nāma*) has the power to connect us with both His form (*rūpa*) and His nature (*svarūpa*). By repetition we can gain His vision (*darśana*) and by contemplation, the realisation of His nature. In the *Geeta* the Lord Himself says, "Amongst all the forms of sacrifice, I am *japa* (*yajñānāṁ japa yajño'smi*)." All the Scriptures and Saints have extolled *japa*, "Undoubtedly, there is nothing which cannot be achieved through *japa* (*Japāt siddhiḥ japāt siddhiḥ japāt siddhir na saṁśayaḥ*)."

Janabai, the great saint of Maharashtra, was once seen arguing that a cow-dung cake was hers when another girl challanged it. It was proved to be hers as the sound, "*Viṭṭhala, Viṭṭhala..*" was emanating from it. She used to chant the name *Viṭṭhala* as she made the cakes!

Though it is so highly praised and recommended, most of us find this practice very difficult. The mind either becomes dull, goes to sleep or remains distracted and uninterested. But with regular practice, done with faith and devotion, its deep and lasting effect can be experienced.

This verse however talks of the *japa* which is neither verbal, silent nor mental. It is not of the nature of conscious repetition or concentration. it requires no rosary, time, place or rules. It happens within each of us irrespective of our caste, creed, colour, nationality, religion or belief. It can never be forgotten, given or taken away. Then what is it?

As we inhale and exhale, there is the natural sound *'sa'* and *'haṁ'*. Together it forms the sound *'so'haṁ'* which is the *mantra* that gets repeated unconsciously and effortlessly as we breathe. This is called *ajapā-japa*. The *Yoga Chudamani Upanishad* says that man breathes 21,600 times each day and repeats the *mantra so'haṁ* as many times through his breathing!

Śaṭśatāni divārātrau sahasrāṇyekaviṁśatiḥ
Etat saṁkhyātmakaṁ mantraṁ jīvo japati sarvadā

This practice consists of becoming aware of one's breathing and connecting ourself to the meaning conveyed by the *mantra 'so'haṁ'*.

So'haṁ means 'That (Truth) I am'. *'Sa'* indicates the infinite reality, the substratum of the entire world. *'Aham'* is the pure unconditioned Self, the Witness of the three states. Through contemplation on the meaning of the two sounds there is the Realisation that I am that infinite Truth. This Realisation frees the person from all limitations and sorrows.

* * *

Can we be happy in ourselves, all by ourselves? The next verse explains how we can do so.

तर्पणं स्वसुखेनैव स्वेन्द्रियाणां प्रतर्पणम् ।
मनसा मन आलोक्य स्वयमात्मा प्रकाशते ॥ ११ ॥

tarpaṇaṁ svasukhenaiva svendriyāṇāṁ pratarpaṇam|
manasā mana ālokya svayamātmā prakāśate|| 11||

11. तर्पणम् = *'Tarpanam'*; एव = is verily; प्रतर्पणम् = the satisfaction; स्व-इन्द्रियाणां = of one's sense organs (of perception and knowledge); स्वसुखेन = by the Bliss of the Self; आलोक्य = having percieved; मनः = the mind; मनसा = by the mind; आत्मा = the Self; प्रकाशते = shines; स्वयम् = by Itself.

> *11. 'Tarpanam' is verily the satisfaction of one's sense organs (of perception and knowledge) by the Bliss of the Self. Having perceived the mind by the mind, the Self shines by Itself.*

We progress faster in life with the good wishes and blessings of our elders. In making others happy, we too become fulfilled. Our grateful remembrance of our ancestors for their contribution in our life is the best way to repay our debt to them (*pitṛ ṛṇa*) and make them happy. Their satisfaction flows to us as blessings. To pass on the great culture that they have given us to the next generation is also very important. For this purpose, as part of the daily *sandhyā* ritual we do *tarpaṇam*—with offering oblations to our ancestors.

All our actions are blessed by the deities who govern various functions and the elements. The Moon (as *devatā*) governs the mind, the Sun God the intellect etc. We invoke their grace and satisfy them, and thereby ourselves, by making offerings to them. This too forms a part of the daily *sandhyāvandanam*.

We are by nature infinite and complete. Not knowing that, we consider ourselves to be the finite body. We therefore always feel a sense of incompleteness (*apūrṇo'ham*), discontentment, a desire to become fulfilled. We try to fill this void by sense gratification or by making others happy. When we enjoy the desired object, there arises a feeling—'enough' (*alaṁ buddhi*) as we are temporarily satisfied (*tṛpto'ham*). Since the objects, our senses and their capacities are finite, our joy too is finite and therefore after a short spell of satisfaction we again feel discontent. Also our joy is dependent on various factors like the availability of the object, condition of the mind and senses, the whims and fancies of others, and other external factors. Thus as long as we seek fulfillment in worldly pursuits, we will never find lasting satisfaction.

What actually happens when one feels satisfied? We find that the senses and the mind become quiet and their craving stops. This state where there is no more desire is what we call satisfaction. Adi Shankaracharya advices the seeker to withdraw the senses from their normal extrovertedness (*āvṛtta cakṣuḥ*). The senses get their power through the backing of the mind. When the mind does not pay attention or brood over what is seen, heard etc. the senses automatically become defunct and quiet. The mind's attention should then be turned to itself (*manasā manȧ ālokya*), towards its own source. In this process, the thoughts cease and the Self which illumines the mind, shines forth (*svayaṁ ātmā prakāśate*). In this state, the mind and senses are completely quietened and there is the experience, 'I am infinite Bliss (*ānando'ham*)', 'I am full and complete (*pūrṇo'ham*)', 'I have done what I need to do (*kṛtakṛtyo'ham*) and attained what I wanted (*prapanīyaṁ prāpto'ham*)'. This is the experience of total satisfaction without any desires (*niraṅkuśo tarpaṇa*). His actions thereafter are never desire-prompted or selfish but spring from true fulfillment and are therefore a blessing to mankind.

"True knowledge is that which quietens the senses (*tad jñānaṁ praśamakaraṁ yad indriyāṇām*)." We spend a large part of our life only in thrilling the mind and entertaining the senses. However, meditation is to withdraw them from extrovert pursuits and see (the Self) without the eye and hear (the Self) without ears. Even its practice gives great peace, then what to speak of its culmination in Realisation!

* * *

Is there a way in which what is given, comes back to us multiplied a thousand fold? The *sadācāra* of *agnihotra* is now being described.

आत्मनि स्वप्रकाशाग्नौ चित्तमेकाहुतिं क्षिपेत्।
अग्निहोत्री स विज्ञेयश्चेतरा नामधारकाः ॥ १२ ॥

ātmani svaprakāśāgnau cittamekāhutiṁ kṣipet।
agnihotrī sa vijñeyaścetarā nāmadhārakāḥ।। 12।।

12. क्षिपेत् = One should offer; चित्तम् = the mind; एक-आहुतिं = as a single oblation; आत्मनि = in the Self; स्व-प्रकाश-अग्नौ = in the self-effulgent fire; सः = he; विज्ञेयः = is to be recognised; अग्निहोत्री = as a performer of *Agnihotra*; च = and; इतराः = all other performers; नामधारकाः = are only for namesake.

12. One should offer the mind as a single oblation in the self-effulgent fire of the Self. He is to be recognised as a performer of Agnihotra and all other performers are only for namesake.

The inert cannot function on its own. It needs the sentient to enliven it. The sentient factors behind the entire inert world and all actions are called the presiding deities (*devatās*). For e.g., the presiding deity of the mind is the moon; and therefore the mentally unstable used to be called 'lunatics'. These presiding deities have been blessing all our actions. It is because of them that the eyes see, ears hear etc. We invoke their extra blessings through worship (*upāsanā*). e.g. May the eyes see better, the mind be more alert etc. One of the powerful forms of *upāsanā* is the daily *agnihotra / homa / havana / yajña* (fire worship).

Fire is the vehicle that carries our offerings to the presiding deity that is worshipped. Fire is kindled in the fire container (*homa kunda*). Special wood of sacred trees and plants is used. Clarified butter (*ghee*) is offered into the fire invoked along with various herbs (*auṣadhi*) and grains (*dhānya*). *Mantras* are chanted invoking the grace of the presiding deities. The gross aspect of what is offered (*āhūti*) burns to become the holy ash which is later distributed as *prasāda* (holy gift). The middle aspect becomes the smoke which purifies the atmosphere. This smoke is also known to cure many physical ailments. The subtle aspect (*arci*) is carried by the fire and conveyed to the presiding deity invoked by the *mantras* chanted once or various times. "Having been thus worshipped, they shower their blessings on the worshipper. Through this mutual give and take, one attains greater success and well-being". —The *Geeta: chapter III.*

Devāḥ-bhāvayatānena te devā bhāvayantu vaḥ.
Parasparaṁ bhāvayantaḥ śreyaḥ param-avāpsyatha.

The *Geeta* describes various forms of spiritual practices as sacrifices (*yajñas*). Some are physical, others are verbal and some purely mental. In each of them we have to sacrifice something lower in order to gain something higher. This is the only way to progress in life. We cannot have our cake and eat it too!

The *yajña* spirit is what is described as *karma yoga*. It is to surrender ones ego (*ahaṁkāra*) and egocentric desires (*svārtha*) and perform actions as a dedication to a higher altar (*arpaṇa buddhi*) and accept what we get as a result of our action as the gift of the Lord (*prasāda buddhi*).

Fire is a purifier (*pāvaka*). It burns away all the rubbish put in it. All our *vāsanās* offered to the Lord are burnt down. Fire melts and purifies the metal heated in it. Even a hard and cruel heart melts and gets purified by the touch or grace of the Lord. This is symbolised in our daily practice through the *agnihotra*.

Some criticise the performance of daily or occasional *yajñas* as a waste of scarce wood, costly clarified butter and edible grains. These criticisms are unreasonable as the good effect of the *yajña* on the individual mind and the body, and the spiritual purification of even the place where it is performed are scientifically proved beyond doubt. It is a strange but true fact that during the Bhopal gas tragedy, one of the only families that remained unaffected in the area close to the gas plant was in a home where *agnihotra* was regularly performed. It is strange indeed that some who vociferously argue against *homas* and the like hardly raise an objection against or to improve the millions who ruin their health in drinking alcohol daily at an unbelievable monetary and psychological cost to so many!

The *Geeta* also says that greater than the fire sacrifice with materials is the one with knowledge (*śreyān-dravyamayād-yajñāj-jñānayajñaḥ parantapa*).

Adi Shankaracharya explains the importance of *yajña* performed with Vedantic vision. The Self is the self-lit and ever-burning fire within the body. It does not ever get blown off or dimmed. It only seems to get covered by the smoke of indiscrimination and false notions. The wind of discrimination and dispassion reveals the Self. It is the ego or the mind (*chittam*) that creates the duality and assumes for itself an identity separate from the Self. This ignorance born ego is to be offered into the fire of the Self. Such an offering can only be made once (*eka āhutim*) as once the ego is destroyed there remains no one and nothing more to offer. "The wise call a person, who has burnt all his ignorance-born actions, *vāsanās* or ego, in the fire of Self-knowledge, as a realised one." (*jñānāgṇi-dagdha-karmāṇaṁ tam-āhu paṇḍitaṁ budhāḥ*)

Lord Vishnu came to King Bali, dressed as a young *brāhmin* and asked for just as much land as his three steps would cover. The king readily promised to do so. The Lord covered the entire earth and heaven in two steps and asked where he could put the third. Bali finally offered his own head (ego or mind) for the Lord to place his foot on, and with that he attained Liberation.

* * *

Is there a way to worship the Lord who dwells within us? The verse explains.

देहो देवालयः प्रोक्तो देही देवो निरञ्जनः।
अर्चितः सर्वभावेन स्वानुभूत्या विराजंते ॥ १३ ॥

deho devālayaḥ prokto dehī devo nirañjanaḥ|
arcitaḥ sarvabhāvena svānubhūtyā virājate|| 13||

13. देहः = The body; प्रोक्तः = is said; देवालयः = to be the temple; देही = the owner of the body; निरञ्जनः = is the pure; देवः = Lord; अर्चितः = when worshipped; सर्वभावेन = with full devotion; विराजते = He shines forth; स्व-अनुभूत्या = by the experience of the Self.

13. *The body is said to be the temple. The owner of the body is the pure Lord. When worshipped with full devotion, He shines forth by the experience of the Self.*

Truth is love. Love always seeks expression. One of its expressions is idolising and worshipping one's ideal. Indians are not 'idol worshippers'. They worship the ideal symbolised in the idol. It is difficult to conceive of the Truth, as it is nameless, formless and devoid of all qualities. The Truth, represented in the idol, is therefore worshipped. In the *Vedic* period the natural forces (sun, space etc.) were the 'idols' worshipped. After the *Purāṇic* period, the idols of the various incarnations of the Lord (Rama, Krishna etc.) came to be worshipped with due rituals. This worship is called *pūjā*. It is a ritualistic worship of the idol of the Lord done with reverence (*pūjya bhāva*). Reverence is the confluence of devotion (*bhakti*), respect (*ādara*) and faith (*śraddhā*) towards the same object or being.

Actions by themselves are inert. It is the intentions and feeling behind them that make them good or bad. In worship too; the *bhāva* or feeling is most important. The *vidhi* or method is secondary when the *bhāva* is strong and pure. Overwhelmed with love, Vidura's wife fed Shri Krishna the banana peel, casting away the fruit. Also we always offer what is best to those we love. In fact we wish to give and keep giving all we have to those we love. If we do not have a lot of the best, we still give what we have. The Lord says, "I gladly accept the devotion with which you offer anything to me, be it a leaf, a flower or just plain water."—*Geeta: chapter IX:26*

However devotion is not natural and spontaneous to all. We need to follow methods of worship, which in time help to cultivate higher feelings. The *Dharma Shāstras* thus give us a step-by-step method of ritualistic worship (*śoḍaśopacāra pūjā*—sixteen step worship).

Indians consider guests as the Lord Himself. Suppose the Lord were to come as an invited guest, what would we do? The *pūjā* (ritualistic worship) is one of the ways by which we express our reverence for the Lord symbolised in the idol, treating Him as our most revered guest.

Before commencing the actual worship, we clean and decorate the altar or temple and gather all the materials required for the worship. We then invoke Shri Ganesha, Shri Sarasvati and Shri Guru without whose blessings nothing is started. We purify the atmosphere (*diśā śuddhi*), seat (*āsana śuddhi*), body (*deha śuddhi*) and mind (*ācamanīyam*), regulate the vital air (*prāṇāyama*) and state the intention of the worship (*saṅkalpa*). We then eagerly await the Guest (Lord) as we meditate (*dhyānam*) on Him. On His arrival, we welcome Him (*āvāhanam*) and offer Him a well-decorated seat (*āsanam*). We wash His feet (*pādyam*) and hands (*arghyam*) and offer Him water to drink (*ācamanīyam*). He is then given a bath (*snānam*) and a special bath (*abhiṣekam*) with materials like honey, milk, curds, tender coconut water, sugarcane juice etc. We adorn Him with the best of clothes (*vastram*) and ornaments (*ābhūṣaṇam*), apply sandal paste (*gandhaṃ*) and vermillion powder (*kumkum*), and offer Him rice (*akṣatā*). We beautify Him with flowers (*puṣpāṇi*) and honour Him with a garland (*puṣpa mālā*). Chanting His names in praise, and with prostration, we offer flowers at His feet (*arcanam*). Thereafter we offer incense (*dhūpaṃ*) and with a lamp illumine His countenance (*dīpam*). We lay out a variety of cooked foods with desserts and fruits (*naivedyam*). Thereafter He is given water for washing and drinking, after which we offer him betel leaves (*tāmbūlam*). We entertain the Lord with devotional songs and dance (*rājopacāra*). Having satisfied Him with good entertainment, in gratitude for having accepted to come, we offer Him a gift (*dakṣiṇā*). We worship Him with the waving of lights before Him (*ārati*) accompanied by the ringing of the bells and the blowing of the conch. We then circumambulate Him (*pradakṣiṇā*) remembering that He is the centre of our life and prostrate ourselves before Him showing our complete surrender. Thereafter we beg forgiveness for any shortcomings on our part, particularly during the *pūjā* and humbly pray to Him to bless us with more faith, devotion, knowledge and dispassion. Finally we bid Him a poignant farewell, inviting Him to grace our altar again. The peace and blessedness felt is internalised (*śānti pāṭha*) and the food that He has eaten (*prasādam*) is partaken of with joy.

Indians, the world over, experience the joy and fulfilment in this ceremony when they entertain great souls (*mahātmās*) in their home. The same is done each day for the idol. This ceremony could be done in just five minutes covering just a few of the steps or elaborately for hours. Devotees even put the Lord to bed each night as part of the *pūjā*. One may witness various kinds of *pūjā* in a temple, or do it daily at home or have special *pūjās* on occasions like birthdays, festivals etc.

God's beautiful creation is made up of the five elements (space, air, fire, water and earth) which have the qualities of sound, touch, colour (form), taste and smell. In the *pūjā*, we offer the Lord the five elements and their qualities—the divine sound of the conch, chanting, music, the *abhiṣeka* with the most sacred materials and the best of clothes, flowers and ornaments of the most beautiful colours and forms, the tastiest of food and divine smelling incense and perfumes. As we offer all this, we remember that we are only giving Him what is actually His (*terā tujhko arpaṇa*). In the *pūjā* therefore, we employ our senses to rejoice and revel in the Lord's creation. This purifies and strengthens the mind with love and faith. Sense pleasures otherwise create binding *vāsanās* (tendencies that in time rule and enslave us).

Pūjā can be performed with the sense of duality of the worshipper and the worshipped or without a sense of duality. The former can be with materials physical (*kāyik*) as described above or mental (*mānasik*). *Mānasik pūjā* of course places no limitations in what can be offered and is much more effective than physical worship. However such a mental *pūjā* is difficult for one who has not practised physical *pūjā* to some extent.

Adi Shankaracharya describes the *pūjā* that is to be performed without duality. The body is revered as the temple of the Lord (*deho devālayaḥ prokto*). The individual (*jīva*) is the worshipper and the Self (*ātmā*) is the Lord within (*jīvo hamsa sadāśivaḥ*). Giving up all false notions and ignorance (*tyajet ajñāna nirmālyam*), the ego surrenders by offering itself to the Self, losing its individuality in the Lord within (*so'ham bhāvena pūjayet*). Thereafter the Self alone shines in all Its glory (*svānubhūtyā virājate*).

* * *

It is said that silence is golden and that meditation is the ultimate spiritual practice, presently much in vogue the world over. The following verse gives the crux of these two important daily practices.

मौनं स्वाध्ययनं ध्यानं ध्येयं ब्रह्मानुचिन्तनम्।
ज्ञानेनेति तयोः सम्यङ्निषेधात्तत्त्वदर्शनम्॥ १४॥

maunaṁ svādhyayanaṁ dhyānaṁ dhyeyaṁ brahmānucintanam।
jñāneneti tayoḥ samyaṅniṣedhāttattvadarśanam।। 14।।

14. मौनम् = Silence; स्वाध्ययनम् = is the study of the Scriptures; ध्यानम् = meditation; ब्रह्म-अनुचिन्तनम् = is the continuous thinking of *Brahman*; ध्येयम् = that which is to be meditated upon; सम्यक्-निषेधात् = by the complete negation; तयोः = of both (study of the Scriptures and the continuous thinking of *Brahman*); ज्ञानेन = by Knowledge; इति = is thus; तत्त्व-दर्शनम् = the vision of the Truth.

14. Silence is the study of the Scriptures. Meditation is the continuous thinking of Brahman which is to be meditated upon. The complete negation of both (the study of the Scriptures and the continuous thinking of Brahman) by Knowlege is the vision of the Truth.

***Mounam* : Silence:** There are four levels of speech (*vāṇī*):

1. ***Parā vāṇī* : Supreme speech:** It is the unmanifest source from which all sounds and words emerge.

2. ***Paśyanti vāṇī* : Seen speech:** When an idea takes shape, the words vaguely gather, giving a more concrete form to the idea. We begin to 'see' the idea, hence *paśyanti*.
3. ***Madhyamā vāṇī* : Middle speech:** Just before we actually speak, the words have crystalised and are clear and in syntax.
4. ***Vaikharī vāṇī* : Spoken speech:** Finally the words are enunciated with the help of the vocal chords.

To not speak, i.e. not express the *vaikharī vāṇī* is called 'verbal silence' (*girā maunam*).

Speech is an important way of self-expression. But to keep silent is also important as it is then that we listen, learn and grow.

'The Creator made silence as a good cover to hide our foolishness (which would otherwise be exposed through words), to be used especially in a gathering of the wise.'

Svāyattam-ekānta-hitaṁ vidhātrā vinirmitaṁ chādadaṁ ajñatāyāḥ.

Viśeṣataḥ sarvavidāṁ samāje vibhūṣaṇaṁ maunaṁ apaṇḍitānām.—Nītī Śatakam

Quarrels end when one becomes silent. One avoids the sin of lying, angry words or insults by keeping quiet. We conserve energy which gets dissipated in fruitless talk by observing silence. It is therefore said, "Silence is the best (solution)—*sabse baḍī cupa,*" and "one should attain everything by silence"—"*maunena sarvārthaṁ sādhayet.*"

The *Geeta* says, "Amongst all the secrets, I (God) am silence." (*maunaṁ caivāsmi guhyānām*). If people could remain silent, secrets would never get revealed., gossip would get no fuel and dirty linen would not be washed in public. However, keeping a sercret requires strength of character and self-control. Hence the *Geeta* classifies silence and self-control as mental austerity (*maunam ātma-vinigrahaḥ... mānasaṁ tapa ucyate*). Kunti did not reveal to Karna that he was her son, the eldest of the Pandavas, till just before the Mahabharata war. Considering himself to be of low birth, he suffered severe insults throughout his life and found himself in the unenviable position of having to fight his own brothers in war. In anger he cursed all women, "May you never be able to keep any secret."

Some take on the vow of silence during meals, whilst worshipping, performing rituals etc. as this keeps their mind focussed on the action performed. Some observe silence for a day, week, month or years. Some even when observing verbal silence communicate through gestures and written words whereas some avoid even eye contact.

Observance of silence makes us realise how much time and energy we normally waste in talking, and that we do not need to speak most of what we do. It empowers our speech and makes it more meaningful. We become more observant, sensitive and recepetive to all that is happening around us. It helps develop self-control and makes us introspective (*sva-adhyayanam*—self-study), quiet and contemplative (*munī bhāva*). Such a mind is then ready for an indepth study of the Scriptures (*svādhyayanam*). Thus regular practice of verbal silence when observed appropriately leads to mental silence (*mānasik maunam*).

The practice of verbal and mental silence leads to the highest form of silence which is the non-dual auspicious silence (*śāntaṁ śivaṁ advaitam*) of our own true nature. That is the state of Realisation from where the mind and speech return without attaining it (*yasmāt vāco nivartante aprāpya manasā saha yan maunaṁ yogīnāṁ gamyam.—Aparokśānūbhūti*).

***Dhyānam* : Meditation:** It comes from the verbal root *dhyai*—to think or dwell upon. It means to focus one's attention on an exalted altar—the Lord/Truth, to the exclusion of all else (*sajātīya vṛtti pravāha*). It can be either on the Lord with form (*saguṇa dhyāna*) or the formless Truth (*nirguṇa dhyāna*). *Saguṇa dhyāna* is meditation on the name (*nāma*), form (*rūpa*), qualities (*guṇa*), sports (*līlā*), or abode (*dhāma*) of the Lord.

Meditation on the formless Truth (*Brahma*) involves owning the Truth as our true nature (*svarūpa*). We first have to ascertain and doubtlessly affirm this. We presently think of ourself only as the body-mind-intellect assemblage. By listening to the words of the Guru (*śravaṇa*) and reflecting on the Truth (*manana*) we understand—'I am the infinite Truth'. This intellectual understanding is thereafter realized through meditation (*anu-cintanam*). This thought is continuously maintained, initially with effort (*virala-cintanam*) and, with practise, effortlessly (*sarala cintanam*). Such effortless awareness of our infinite nature is called meditation (*dhyānaṁ nāma svarūpasya sahajaṁ bhānam ucyate*).

Usually what goes on in the name of meditation is the practice of meditation postures, breathing exercises or repetition of *mantras* which render the mind peaceful. Such practices are definitely aids to meditation but not proper meditation. Vedantic meditation is an independent state attained by the thought 'I am the infinite Truth' (*brahmaivāsmi iti sadvṛttyā nirālambatayā sthitiḥ dhānaśabdena vikhyātā*).

* * *

Food is an all-consuming passion for many. Some live to eat, drink and be merry. What should our attitude be towards this daily act of eating and towards all that we get as simple pleasures of life?

अतीतानागतं किञ्चिन्न स्मरामि न चिन्तये ।
रागद्वेषविना प्राप्तं भुञ्जाम्यत्र शुभाशुभम् ॥ १५ ॥

atītānāgataṁ kiñcin-na smarāmi na cintaye|
rāgadveṣavinā prāptaṁ bhuñjāmyatra
śubhāśubham|| 15||

15. न स्मरामि = I do not remember; न चिन्तये = I do not brood over; न किञ्चित् = even a wee bit; अतीत-अनागतम् = about the past and the future (experiences); भुञ्जामि = I enjoy; अत्र = here; शुभ-अशुभम् = pleasant or unpleasant; प्राप्तम् = that is attained; राग-द्वेष-विना = without likes and dislikes.

15. I do not remember nor do I brood over even a wee bit on the past and future (experiences). I enjoy both the pleasant and the unpleasant that is attained without likes and dislikes.

Just a couple of generations back, a 'two full-meals' day was practised in India. After completing one's morning spiritual practices, one ate a wholesome meal before going to work. On returning from work and completing the evening spiritual practices, one ate another wholesome meal.

The cooked food is first offered to the Lord. The offered food is then eaten as *prasāda*—a holy gift from the Lord. Before sitting for a meal, we wash our hands and feet. It is unhealthy to stand, walk, recline or lie down and eat. We should give our undivided attention to what we do and so we should avoid watching TV, reading or having heated discussions whilst eating.

Eating itself is considered as an act of (fire) worship (*pūjā* or *prāṇāgnihotram*) wherein food is offered to the Lord within, who resides as the digestive fire (*ahaṁ vaiśvānaro bhūtvā prāṇināṁ deham āśritaḥ*).

Therefore with water in hand we chant:

brahmārpaṇaṁ brahmahaviḥ brahmāgnau
brahmaṇāhutam
brahmaiva tena gantavyaṁ brahmakarma samādhinā.

"The Truth is the oblation, the clarified butter and the fire. The Truth alone is reached by him who sees the Supreme in all actions."

The food is encircled with water and drunk with the words *satyaṁ tvā ṛtena parisiñcāmi* and *amṛtopastaraṇam asi svāhā*. "We purify the offering with Truth (water). Thou art the nectarine covering (to the food)."

Before we partake of the food, five morsels (*grāsa*) are placed outside the plate, acknowledging the debt owed by us as follows:

1. Our debt to the Divine forces (*deva ṛṇa*): for their benign grace and protection,
2. Our debt to our ancestors (*pitṛ ṛṇa*): for giving us their lineage and family culture,
3. Our debt to the sages (*ṛṣi ṛṇa*): as our religion and the culture has been revealed to them and then maintained and handed down to us by them,
4. Our debt to our fellow beings (*manuṣya ṛṇa*): the society without whose support we could not live as we do, and
5. Our debt to other living beings and the environment (*bhūta ṛṇa*): for serving us selflessly.

Thereafter, the Lord who exists also as the five life-giving physiological functions (the respiration, excretion, circulation, digestion and reversal systems) is offered food by taking in five morsels with the words *prāṇāya svāhā, apānāya svāhā, vyānāya svāhā, udānāya svāhā, samānāya svāhā, brahmaṇe svāhā*. Thereafter the food is eaten as *prasāda*—blessed food.

On completion of the meal, we sip water which is first held in the palm and consecrated with the words *amṛtam apidhānam asi svāhā*—Thou art the nectarine covering (to the food). The food is thus meant to give us longevity, a pure mind, strength, nourishment, health, joy and love. After a wholesome meal, we should walk for a minimum of 100 steps and then relax a while by lying on the left side. Sitting in *vajrāsana* for a few minutes after a meal is also recommended for easy digestion.

But what should be our attitude towards the food we eat or in a wider sense, in facing any circumstance that comes to us? "Food (pleasures) is the medicine for the disease of hunger (desires) (*bhikṣauṣadhaṁ bhujyatām*)." Hence we should eat in limited and appropriate quantity and at the prescribed time. "Do not crave for tasty food (pleasures), but be content with whatever is ordained (*svādvannaṁ na tu yācyatām vidhivaśāt prāptena santuṣyatām*)." "A wise man is content with whatever comes his way (*santuṣṭo yena kenacit*)." The wise do not waste time regretting or remembering the past, or worrying or dreaming about the future. They remain focussed in the 'here and now'. They cheerfully accept and enjoy all that comes to them in the present. They have no likes, dislikes, areas of insistence or prejudices against anyone (*budheḥ phalaṁ anāgraham*) and they do not categorise circumstances as conducive/non-conducive, auspicious/inauspicious or desirable/

undesirable (*śubha-aśubhaṁ parityāgi*). Such people are easily satisfied (*alpa bhogena tuṣyati*) and ever happy.

A king saw a one-eyed man before starting his hunting trip. He came back without a catch that day and blamed his chance seeing of the one-eyed man for his ill-luck and failure. He ordered that the man be hanged. As his last wish, the man asked to see the king. The king reluctantly agreed. On seeing the king, the condemned man said, "Seeing my face you could not get a kill on your hunting trip. But seeing your face will cause my death. I wonder whose face is more unlucky and inauspicious!" Wisdom dawned on the king and the man was released.

* * *

We need to qualify in order to run in the Olympics. What are the qualifications required for gaining Supreme Knowledge?

अभयं सर्वभूतानां ज्ञानमाहुर्मनीषिणः ।
निजानन्दे स्पृहा नान्ये वैराग्यस्यावधिर्मतः ॥ १६ ॥

abhayaṁ sarvabhūtānāṁ jñānamāhurmanīṣiṇaḥ|
nijānande spṛhā nānye vairāgyasyāvadhirmataḥ|| *16*||

16. मनीषिणः = Wise men; आहुः = describe; ज्ञानम् = as Knowledge; अभयम् = fearlesness; सर्व-भूतानाम् = towards all beings. स्पृहा = The yearning; निज-अनन्दे = for the

Bliss of the Self; न = not; अन्ये = for anything else; मतः = is considered; अवधिः = as the limit; वैराग्यस्य = of dispassion.

16. *Wise men describe fearlessness towards all beings as Knoweldge. The yearning for the Bliss of the Self and not for anything else is considered as the limit of dispassion.*

***Vairāgyam* : Dispassion:**

Vedanta enumerates the four-fold qualifications to gain the Supreme Knowledge as discrimination (*viveka*), dispassion (*vairāgya*), the six-fold wealth (*ṣaṭ sampatti*) [viz. control over the mind (*śama*), control over the sense organs of action and perception (*dama*), withdrawal from extrovertedness (*uparama*), forbearance (*titikṣā*), faith (*śraddhā*) and self-absorption (*samādhāna*)] and an intense desire for Liberation (*mumukṣutvam*). Of all these, dispassion and the intense desire for Liberation are the most important.

"Following one's duties according to one's stage and status in life, performing austerities and the grace of God, give rise to the four-fold qualifications of dispassion etc."

svavarṇāśrama-dharmeṇa tapasā hari-toṣanāt
sādhanaṁ prabhavet puṁsāṁ vairāgyādi-catuṣṭayam—
Aparokṣānubhūti

"Dispassion is aided by discrimination and vice versa. Usually they go together but in some, one or the other is seen."

vairāgya-bodho-paramāḥ sahāyāste parasparam
prāyeṇa saha vartante viyujyante kvacit-kvacit— *Pañcadaśi IV.276*

Pleasures are finite, and yet attained only through great efforts, they leave our mind and senses fatigued and weak, make us dependent and discontent, create more desires, attachments and agitation and ultimately give sorrow alone. When we are able to see their limitation (*doṣa dṛṣṭi*), we get detached from them. Dispassion is not hatred towards things and beings, but an end to the superimposition of happiness on them and the consequent indifference towards what was earlier thought to be pleasurable objects (*abhāva buddhe audāṣīyam*). Pujya Gurudev Swami Chinmayananda, whilst consoling a blind man assured him, "You are not missing much, my friend. There is nothing in this world worth seeing." One with strong dispassion is not lured even by heavenly pleasures or divine powers. Dispassion results in independencee (*svatantratā*), fearlessness (*vairāgyam eva abhayam*) and mental peace (*tyāgāt śāntir-anantaram*).

Supreme Knowledge is gained by *śravaṇa* (listening to the Scriptures), *manana* (reflecting on them) and *nidhidhyāsana* (meditation). Knowledge enables us to discriminate clearly between the Real and unreal (*sat-asat*), the sentient and the inert (*cetan-jaḍa*), the Self and the not-Self (*ātmā-anātmā*). We can thereafter renounce all that is unreal, inert and not the Self and realise our true nature. This results in Liberation (*mukti*) wherein there is no more the chance of re-identifying with the not-Self (*punaḥ granthe anudaya*).

***Jñānam* : Knowledge:**

Fear arises only when there is a notion of otherness (*yad idam antaraṁ kurute atha tasya bhayam bhavati*). With Realisation, we know that the Self in me is the Self in all and all notions of otherness end. Therefore one becomes fearless. 'Fear is of the unknown.' "Knowing the Self all else becomes as well known (*yad vijñāne sarvaṁ vijñātaṁ bhavati*)." One fears losing a desired object, name, fame etc. In the gain of the infinite Self all pleasures are included and therefore man becomes fearless.

To give food in charity is noble (*anna dānaṁ mahādānam*). However, to teach a profession is far nobler (*vidyā dānaṁ mahattaraḥ*) as man can then earn his own bread and butter. But to bestow fearlessness by giving the Knowledge of the Self is the noblest form of giving (*abhaya dānaṁ mahattamaḥ*) as it enables man to become fulfilled in every way. Shri Rama took a vow when Vibhishana surrendered to Him, "When a devotee surrenders to Me with the words 'I am yours', I will give him the 'boon of fearlessness' from all beings."

Sukṛdapi prapannāya tavāsmi iti yacaka
Abhayaṁ sarva bhūtebhyo dadāmi etat vratam mama

None who receive such a boon from the Lord need to ask for anything ever again!

* * *

To hit the bull's eye, we need to initially clean, oil and load the rifle, and thereafter focus, aim and steady it. Similarly once the mind is, to some extent, endowed with the four-fold qualification, what is to be done for Self-realisation is now explained. These are called *antaraṅga sādhanā* —the inner fine-tuning.

वेदान्तैः श्रवणं कुर्यान्मननं चोपपत्तिभिः ।
योगेनाभ्यसनं नित्यं ततो दर्शनमात्मनः ॥ १७ ॥

vedāntaiḥ śravaṇaṁ kuryān-mananaṁ copapattibhiḥ |
yogenābhyasanaṁ nityaṁ tato darśanamātmanaḥ || 17 ||

17. कुर्यात् = One should do; श्रवणम् = *śravaṇam* (listening); वेदान्तैः = with the *Upanishads*; च = and; मननम् = *mananam* (reflection); उपपत्तिभिः = by rational analysis; अभ्यसनम् = *abhyāsam* (practice); नित्यम् = (is to

be done) always; योगेन = by *yoga;* ततः = thereafter (arises); दर्शनम् = the vision; आत्मनः = of the Self.

17. *One should listen to the Upanishads and do reflection with rational analysis. Practice is to be done always by Yoga. Then there arises the vision of the Self.*

The Scriptures say that the Self should be realised. In order to do so one should listen, reflect and meditate (*Ātmā va are draṣṭavyaḥ, śrotavyaḥ mantavyaḥ, nididhyāsitavyaḥ*). A pure, subtle and concentrated mind is required for this fine-tuning and Realisation.

***Vedāntaiḥ śravaṇaṁ kuryāt* :** The portion of the *Vedas* that talks about the knowledge of the Self, the ultimate goal of life, the very essence of the Scriptures is called Vedanta. We should listen to Vedanta from a qualified Master who is both learned and wise (*śrotriya brahmaniṣṭha*). Various Masters describe the Scriptrues and various topics in different ways (*ekaṁ sat viprā bahudhā vadanti*). By *śravaṇa* we are able to resolve all the apparent differences and understand the underlying essence of the Scriptures. To ascertain the purport of the Scriptures as— 'the Truth alone is real, the world is an illusion and that the individual is in essence the infinite Truth alone' (*'brahma satyaṁ jagat mithyā jīvo brahmaiva nā paraḥ'*), is called *śravaṇa*. If the mind of the seeker is mature then Realisation (*aparokṣānubhūti*) takes place by *śravaṇa* alone as in the case of King Parikshit. However, in the case of the majority, indirect knowledge (*parokṣa jñāna*) alone takes place. For some even that does not happen due to distracted listening or lack of faith (*parokṣa-jñānaṁ aśraddhā prati badhnāti netarat*). We need to have faith in the ability and nobility of the Master and in the validity of the Scriptrues. This will enable us to ascertain the import of the Scriptrues (*śraddhāvān labhate jñānam*).

Mananaṁ upapattibhiḥ : To 'realise' the knowledge ascertained (*parokṣa jñāna*) as one's own direct experience (*aparokṣa jñāna*) is the purpose of *mananam* (reflection). There are contradictions in the Knowledge of the Scriptures and one's own experiences. To us the world seems real and the Self is considered finite and changing. The Scriptures say the opposite. Independent and logical reflection resolves such contradictions and our knowledge becomes clear and doubtless. 'Lack of thinking, incomplete thinking or wrong thinking are obstacles in the path to Realisation (*avicāro'parokṣasya jñānasya pratibandhakaḥ*)'. Avoiding the pitfalls of wrong logic we should reflect deeply, completely and according to the guidance of the Scriptures (*duṣtarkyāt suviramyatāṁ śrutimatas-tarko'nusandhiyatām*). For a mature seeker *manana* itself results in Realisation. However for the majority, the tendencies of the past (*vāsanā*) are strong, and so the identification with the body (*viparīta bhāvanā*) is not easily destroyed. We therefore have to meditate.

Yogena abhyasanaṁ nityaṁ : *Nididhyāsanam* is to meditate on the Knowledge, made clear and doubtless through reflection. It is to own one's own nature, or to bring in the thought 'I am the infinite Truth alone'. "Regular concentrated practise over a long period of time, with due respect and importance results in firm abidance in the Self (*dīrgha-kāla nairontaryaṁ satkāra-āsevita dṛḍha-bhūmī*)." The false notion, 'I am the body' is removed by consistent and focussed practise of the thought 'I am the infinite Truth'. "Concentration if not already achieved through worship of the Lord, can be attained through the practise of meditation."

Viparīta bhāvaṇeyaṁ ekāgrāt sa nivartate
Tattvopadeśāt prāgeva bhavatyetad-upāsanāt.

The obstacles to Self-realisation are attachments to pleasures, dullness of the intellect, false logic, false notions and insistences.

Pratibandho vartamāno viṣayāsakti lakṣaṇaḥ
Prajñāṁ-āndhyaṁ kutarkaśca viparyaya-durāgrahaḥ.

Attachment to pleasure can be removed by self-control, dullness of the intellect by *śravaṇa*, false logic by *manana*, and the last two by *nididhyāsana*.

* * *

The following two verses establish the vital role of the *Guru* and the Scriptures in gaining Self-realisation.

शब्दशक्तेरचिन्त्यत्वात् शब्दादेवापरोक्षधीः ।
सुषुप्तः पुरुषो यद्वत् शब्देनैवावबुद्ध्यते ॥ १८ ॥

śabdaśakteracintyatvāt śabdādevāparokṣadhīḥ।
suṣuptaḥ puruṣo yadvat śabdenaivāvabuddhyate।। 18।।

18. अपरोक्षधीः = One becomes a person of direct experience; शब्दाद् एव = from the words (of the Scriptures); अचिन्त्यत्वात् = because of the unfathomable; शब्द-शक्तेः = power of words (the Scriptures); यद्-वत् = just as; सुषुप्तः = the sleeping; पुरुषः = person; अवबुद्ध्यते = awakens; एव = by the very; शब्देन = words (of another).

18. One becomes a person of direct experience through the words of the Scriptrues because of the unfathomable power of the Scriptures just as the sleeping person awakens by the very words (of another).

Man-made literature, discoveries and inventions can have the following defects:

1. ***Bhrama*: Mistaken notion:** Individual's likes and dislikes cause prejudices and opinions which could be passed off as true knowledge. Also cultural, educational and economical conditions cause a bias which affects true knowledge.

2. ***Pramāda*****: Inadvertance:** To err is human. Grammatical errors, mistakes in words, syntax and connotations are possible in man-made literature and affect knoweldge. Erring can even be at the level of theories and concepts which is why science repeatedly disproves its own earlier theories and knowledge.

3. ***Karaṇa apāṭava*****: Limitation of the instruments:** Our perception and understanding is conditioned by our senses and external instruments and our mind and its capacities. Eg. sunset, flat earth, stationary earth etc. are solidly percieved knowledge but far from the truth due to the limitations of our perception.

4. ***Vipralipsā*****: Wrong intentions:** A person's greed for money and desire for pleasure, name and fame could result in deceit and cover-up of limitations in the written word or true knowledge. Even the daily news we read is often interpreted according to the ideology of the publishers.

The *Vedas* are not man-made (*apauruśeya*) and therefore do not have the above mentioned defects. They are the compilation of knowledge 'realised by great sages in their seat of meditation as 'revealed words'. Veda Vyasa is the compiler-cum-editor of the *Vedas* and not its composer as is mistaken by some.

The world is experienced by us through direct perception (eyes, ears, nose, skin, tongue) (*pratyakṣa pramāṇa*), inference (*anumāna pramāṇa*) or through words which are heard or read (*laukika śabda pramāṇa*). The Truth/Self is beyond the perview of perception, words or thoughts. It cannot be established by human logic or experimentation. The *Vedas* reveal that Truth/Self, and hence are the valid means (*apauruṣeya śabda pramāṇa*) for Self-realisation. Their knowledge stands uncontradicted by any other means of knowledge, and hence Vedantic knowledge is the uncontradicted means (*prabala pramāṇa*) for Self-realisation.

Words describe an object or concept in terms of

- Species (*jāti*)—dog, monkey etc.
- Qualities (*guṇa*)—fat man, fast food etc.
- Function (*kriyā*)—lawyer, running boy etc.
- Relation (*saṁbandha*)—sister's father-in-law etc.

The Truth/Self is beyond such description as it does not belong to a species, is unique, attributeless, actionless and relationless.

The *Vedas* only 'indicate' the Truth. When the seeker meditates on the Truth indicated, he 'realises' It.

How far is one who is asleep from the waker? There is no gap of time and space between the sleeper and the waker. There where the 'sleeper' is, the 'waker' is. The sleeper alone is the waker. We, the individuals experiencing this world, have been in the sleep of ignorance of our own true nature from innumerable lifetimes (*anādi māyayā suptaḥ jīvaḥ*). We do not have to gain our own nature in terms of time and space. All we have to do is to awaken, i.e. know that we ourselves are the infinite Self. If not awakened by another's prodding, we may continue to sleep for innumerable more lifetimes. The words of the Scriptures spoken by a compassionate Master have the power to prod us and awaken us to our divine infinite Nature.

Presently, in the state of ignorance, our 'I-thought' (*ahaṁ vṛtti*) is well connected with the body and a name given to it. When one addresses a sleeping man by his name, the dormant 'I-thought' awakes, identifies with the individual and he awakens. The mature seeker who has ascertained that 'I' am not the body, when addressed by the Master as the infinite Self, identifies with the Truth and 'realises' It.

Yeṣāṁ vṛttiḥ sama vṛddha paripakva ca sā punaḥ
Te vai sadbrahmatāṁ prāpta netare śabdavādinaḥ

Even when called softly, a man who is almost awake, gets up immediately. Another who is fast asleep takes repeated calling, whilst it is almost impossible to awaken one who is in a heavy alcohol-induced sleep. Similarly the mature seeker awakens immediately. Others take longer.

"The Self is not gained through excellent oratory (words), by committing the Scriptures to memory (words) or by repeated listening to discourses (words). One who chooses to know alone knows." (*Nāyam ātmā pravacanena labhyaḥ na medhayā na bahudhā śrutena. Yam eva eṣa vṛṇte tena labhya*). The words of the Scriptures if not understood properly, could cause great confusion and misunderstanding (*śabda-jālaṁ mahāraṇyaṁ citta-bhramaṇa kāraṇam*) and thus the very important role of the Guru in Self-realisation.

* * *

The role of the *Guru* is further elaborated.

आत्मानात्मविवेकेन ज्ञानं भवति निश्चलम् ।
गुरुणा बोधितः शिष्यः शब्दब्रह्मातिवर्तते ॥ १९ ॥

ātmānātmavivekena jñānaṁ bhavati niścalam|
guruṇā bodhitaḥ śiṣyaḥ śabdabrahmātivartate|| 19||

19. ज्ञानम् = Knowledge; भवति = becomes; निश्चलम् = steady; आत्म-अनात्म-विवेकेन = by the discrimination between the Self and the not-Self; शिष्यः = the disciple; बोधितः = who is taught; गुरुणा = by the teacher; अतिवर्तते = transcends; शब्द-ब्रह्म = the *Vedas*.

19. Knowledge becomes steady by the discrimination between the Self and the not-Self. The disciple who is taught by the teacher transcends the Vedas.

Right from childhood, the Teacher plays an important role in gaining all knowledge. All worldly knowledges and skills are acquired, fine-tuned and mastered under the guidance of a teacher. Spiritual knowledge is the subtlest of all knowledges. There are greater chances of not understanding or misunderstanding it, if read and studied by oneself. The confused person may not even realise that he is so and may teach and lead others to confusion like the blind leading the blind (*andhenaiva nīyamāna yathāndhāḥ*). Therefore we are cautioned that "even a learned man or scholar should not enquire into Self-knowledge independently (without the guidance of a qualified and wise teacher)." (*śāstrajño'pi svātantreṇa brahma-anveṣaṇaṁ na kuryāt*)

The Master may be great, but the seeker must accept him as his *'Guru'* for his words to be effective. Arjuna knew Shri Krishna since his childhood and considred Him as his close friend, relative, someone who had miraculous powers and would always help in times of trouble. It was only when Arjuna told Shri Krishna, "I am your disciple, I surrender to You, please teach me," that the Lord gave him spiritual Knowledge. Arjuna thereafter declares that by the grace (words) of the Lord, all his delusions have been destroyed and he was truly enlightened.

The words of the Scriptures help us discriminate between the Self and the not-Self. By giving up the identification with the not-Self, we are able to abide in the Self (*nirmohatve niścalatattvam*) which in turn leads to Liberation (*niścalatattve jīvan-muktiḥ*). Like the boat that is abandoned on reaching the other shore, the seeker with the help of the Scriptures as taught by the *Guru* transcends all words and thoughts (*tatra vedo avedo bhavati*).

* * *

The discrimination between the Self and not-Self was indicated as a means to Self-realisation in the previous verse. It is now explained how we can do so.

न त्वं देहो नेन्द्रियाणि न प्राणो न मनो न धीः ।
विकारित्वात् विनाशित्वात् दृश्यत्वाच्च घटो यथा ॥ २० ॥

na tvaṁ deho nendriyāṇi na prāṇo na mano na dhīḥ |
vikāritvād-vināśitvāt dṛśyatvācca ghaṭo yathā || 20 ||

20. त्वम् = You (are); न = not; देहः = the body; न = not; इन्द्रियाणि = the organs of perception and action; न = not; प्राणः = the vital-airs; न = not; मनः = the mind; न = not; धीः = the intellect; विकारित्वात् = for they undergo modifications; विनाशित्वात् = they are

perishable; च = and; दृश्यत्वात् = are seen; यथा = just as; घटः = a pot.

20. *You are not the body, not the organs of perception and action, not the vital-airs, not the mind, not the intellect—for just as a pot, they undergo modifications, are perishable and are seen.*

To many who study, listen, discuss or give discourses on Vedanta, it becomes an initellectual workout, a *sātvik* entertainment or 'time-pass', or of scholarly interest. Therefore some label them as 'dry intellectuals' (*śuṣka vedāntī*). Such people miss out on the great Bliss of Realisation and remain satisfied by the few intellectual thrills they get. The following thoughts should lead us to Realisation and not remain an intellectual exercise.

'I' am the centre of my existence. Who am 'I' is the fundamental question of Vedanta, the answer to which is the Supreme Knowledge and Realisation of the very puspose of existence. It is important to first remove all the false notions about ourselves. Hence what 'I' am not is first explained through an example.

The potter makes a pot from clay. The clay undergoes many changes of form and size to become the pot. Thereafter the pot ages, cracks and finally breaks to be then discarded. It merges back into the earth from which it emerged. 'I' the experiencer of birth, changes and death of the pot, remain ever different from the pot. Maintaining my own independent existence and remaining unaffected by it, I use and discard the pot.

***Na tvaṁ dehaḥ*—You are not the gross body:** Right from birth, I have identified with my body, senses, physiological functions and mind. I have been told and taught by everyone that I am the body with a name given to it, that I am related to all that is related to the body like my toys, my home, my parents etc. We are now asked to question this belief. Am I really this body?

Like the pot, this gross body too is made up of the five elements (space, air, fire, water and earth). It is born, grows, ages and finally perishes to merge with the elements. I nourish and groom it, admire it and use it to transact with the world. The body being changing and perishable just like the pot that I experience and use, how can it not be different from me? How can the experiencer be the experiencedor the user be the used? I may have a closer affinity for the body as it 'seems' to be closer to me, but still, it cannot be mistaken for 'me'.

***Na indriyāṇi*—not the senses:** Similarly I experience the changes in the sense organs of action and perception. "My eye-sight has improved after the cataract operation. Earlier my vision was almost nil."

I, remaining the same, experience those changes and am therefore different from the senses.

***Na prāṇaḥ*—not the vital air:** The five physiological functions (respiration, excretion, digestion, circulation and reversal) also change with time, place and age. We feel more hungry in colder climates and digest faster when young. I can observe the changing pattern of my breathing with the change in my moods and increased heart beat after a brisk walk. I, the observer, am surely different from the observed.

***Na manaḥ*—not the mind:** The mind is a flow of innumerable thought modifications (*vṛtti*), at times calm, sometimes agitated and gurgling, sometimes dull and meandering, at other times stormy and uncontrollable. 'I' know the various thought modifications of my mind intimately. They are with me from the time I awake till they finally become dormant at night. If I were the mind, I would be ever changing even as I read this. Then who am I—the previous thought or the present one? How can these innumerable thought modifications and their fleeting existence be me, who is ever present?

***Na dhī*—not the intellect:** The mind and the intellect are both thought modifications. They are named differently according to their nature and function. Thoughts in a state of fluctuation are termed the mind, and in a state of decision, the intellect. Emotions are called mind, whereas ideas and concepts, the intellect. Perceptions are the mind, and cognition is the intellect and so on. Just as the mind is not me, the intellect too cannot be me.

It is thus proved and left to be realised that 'I' the seer, knower, observer and experiencer is the unchanging one, and different from the seen, known, observed and experienced, which are many and changing.

* * *

After negating all that I am not, nothing seems to remain. But I do exist, and cannot therefore be a void or non-existence. Then who am I?

विशुद्धं केवलं ज्ञानं निर्विशेषं निरञ्जनम्।
यदेकं परमानन्दं तत्त्वमस्यद्वयं परम्॥ २१॥

viśuddhaṁ kevalaṁ jñānaṁ nirviśeṣaṁ nirañjanam|
yadekaṁ paramānandaṁ tattvamasyad-
vayaṁ param|| 21||

21. यत् = That which; विशुद्धम् = is extremely pure; केवलम् = free of differences; ज्ञानम् = (of the nature of) knowledge; निर्विशेषम् = without attributes; निरञ्जनम् = without impurities; एकम् = one; परम-आनन्दम् = supreme Bliss; अद्वयम् = non-dual; परम् = supreme; तत् = That; त्वम् = thou; असि = art.

21. *That which is extremely pure, free of differences, (of the nature of) knowledge, without attributes, without impurities, the one supreme Bliss, non-dual Supreme—'That thou art'.*

None can ever deny their own existence or experience their own absense. 'I am' and 'I know' that I am. Negating all the attributes of the body, mind etc., can I not arrive at who I am?

Viśudhaṁ jñānam **:** The body is inert and impure (*deho māṁsamayo'śuciḥ*). Who can deny that considering the amount of time spent each day to keep it clean and groomed? 'I' am pure Consciousness and most auspicious (*ātmā jñānamayo puṇyaḥ*).

Kevalam **:** One of the ways the body is categorised is according to species, e.g. man, monkey etc. There also exist differences within a species, e.g. chimpanzee, orangutan etc. Within each body again there are different limbs and their functions, e.g. nose for breathing and smelling, legs for walking etc. But 'I' in my real nature do not belong to any species, am undifferentiated, devoid of parts, actionless and therefore free from all differences.

Nirviśeṣam **:** Each body, mind etc. has its own special quality and uniqueness e.g. one can sing and another dance, one is brave and another strong.

'I' am unique in the sense that 'I' have no qualities at all and so am undistinguishable.

Nirañjanam : The body and mind get affected, and influenced by their surroundings (*saṁga doṣa*). 'I' remain ever pure, even though I am ever present in the world of happenings and turmoil.

Ekaṁ, paramānandaṁ, advayam, param : The conditions of the body, mind etc. vary. They are limited by many factors, suffer and cause suffering and always transact in the realm of duality. 'I' am one, non-dual and unconditioned, and therefore of the nature of supreme Bliss.

* * *

Can we realise our true nature only when we transcend all words and thoughts? Is denying all words and thoughts the only way to experience the Self? Is the Self realised only when all thoughts end?

शब्दस्याद्यन्तयोः सिद्धं मनसोऽपि तथैव च ।
मध्ये साक्षितया नित्यं तदेव त्वं भ्रमं जहि ॥ २२ ॥

śabdasyādyantayoḥ siddhaṁ manaso'pi tathaiva ca |
madhye sākṣitayā nityaṁ tadeva tvaṁ
bhramaṁ jahi || 22 ||

22. सिद्धम् = That which is known; आदि-अन्तयोः = in both, the beginning and the end; शब्दस्य = of the

sound (word); तथा एव च = and also; मनसः अपि = of the mind; मध्ये = in the middle (i.e. when the mind exists); नित्यम् = that which ever (exists); साक्षितया = as the Witness; तत् = that; एव = verily; त्वम् = are you. जहि = Destroy; भ्रमम् = the delusion.

22. *That which is known in both the beginning and the end of sound (word), and also during the beginning and the end of thoughts, and that which ever exists as the Witness during the existence of the mind, that verily are you. Destroy the delusion.*

All perceptions, including words and sounds are experienced by us as thought modifications (*vṛtti*). Thoughts arise and disappear at a rapid rate giving us the impression that they are always there. Their momentary existence is experienced by me when they come into my field of awareness. I witness both the presence and absence of thoughts and therefore exist before and after them. They change, I remain the same. I am ever present as the Consciousness that witnesses all thought modifications.

The practice of remaining as a Witness (*sākśī bhāva*) culminates in Realisation. Just as a man sits on a bank of a river and watches the flow of water, remaining detatched and unaffected, we should watch the flow of thoughts. There should be no attempt to connect or understand thoughts, push out or indulge in thoughts, give importance or label thoughts, give momentum or attempt to ignore thoughts, desire or reject thoughts. We should just remain as a Witness to thoughts. Such an attitude is advised as a meditation technique, which can be practiced even during our daily transactions with the world.

We are normally troubled by our thougths and the words of others. Our meditation gets disturbed by outside noise and our own distracted mind. We are asked to stay unperturbed by them and remain as the awareness that illumines all thoughts. "Thoughts spring from an unknown source and again disappear into the unknown. They are neither you nor yours, nor do you belong to them. Then why should they trouble you?"

Adarśanāt āpatitaḥ punaścādarśanaṁ gataḥ
Na sa tava na tasya tvaṁ vṛthā kiṁ paritapyase.

"That which is not there in the beginning and the end, is not really in the middle also, except for namesake."—*na yat purastāt uta yannapaścād madhye ca tanna vyapadeśamātram.*

"That which existed in the past (before) and will exist in the future (after) also exists in the present (middle)."

ādāvante ca yannāsti vartamāne'pi tattathā.

Knowing this we should give up the delusion that I am the ever-changing, appearing and disappearing thoughts and remain as the ever present Witness Consciousness.

* * *

What is my relation with God/Truth? Am I a part of Him, apart from Him, or one with Him? The following verse answers this question.

स्थूलवैराज्ययोरैक्यं सूक्ष्महैरण्यगर्भयोः ।
अज्ञानमाययोरैक्यं प्रत्यग्विज्ञानपूर्णयोः ॥ २३ ॥

sthūla-vairājyayor-aikyaṁ sūkṣma-hairaṇyagarbhayoḥ |
ajñāna-māyayor-aikyaṁ pratyag-vijñāna-pūrṇayoḥ || 23 ||

23. ऐक्यम् = There is identity; स्थूल-वैराज्ययोः = between the individual gross-body and the total gross-body; सूक्ष्म-हैरण्यगर्भयोः = between the individual subtle-body and the total subtle-body; ऐक्यम् = there is identity; अज्ञान-माययोः = between the individual causal-body and the total causal-body; प्रत्यग्विज्ञान-पूर्णयोः = between (individual) Consciousness and total Consciousness.

23. *There is identity between the individual gross-body and the total gross-body and between the individual subtle-body and the total subtle-body. There is also identity between the individual causal body and the*

total causal body and between individual Consciousness and total Consciousness.

Each of us have three bodies (gross, subtle and causal) with which we go through the three states of consciousness (waking, dream and deep sleep) all through our life.

Individual Gross body: It is made up of the five grossified elements (*pañcīkṛta pañca-mahābhūtaiḥ kṛtam*), constitutes the perceived body made up of various limbs, is born as a result of actions done in the past (*sat-karma janyam*) and is a counter through which all worldly transactions take place (*bhoga-āyatanam*).

Individual Subtle body: It is made up of the five subtle elements (*apañcīkṛta pañcamahābhūtaiḥ kṛtam*), constitutes the five sense organs of action, five sense organs of perception, five vital airs or physiological functions and the four types of thought modifications. It is the seat of experience like joy, sorrow etc. (*bhoga sādhanam*) and is born as a result of past actions (*sat-karma janyam*). It is the medium that manifests Consciousness as life. In its absence, the body is called 'dead'. The gross body cannot function without the presence of the subtle body.

Individual Causal body: It consists of the unmanifest inherent tendencies (*vāsanās*) and is the cause of the other two bodies. It is experienced as ignorance (*ajñāna*) in the deep sleep state.

The individual identified with each of the body is called *'viśva'*, *'taijasa'* and *'prājña'* respectively.

Total gross, subtle and causal bodies: The entire universe consisting of innumerable cosmoses constitutes the total gross body of the Lord. The total thought content and vital airs present in the universe is the total subtle body of the Lord. The total causal body is the infinite power of the Lord (*māyā*) which has the potential to create innumerable cosmoses. The Truth identified with each of the three bodies is called *Virāṭ*, *Hiraṇyagarbha* and *Īśvara* respectively.

The totality being infinite, is much more than the sum of individuals, the finite.

The concept of the totality exists only with respect to the individuality. The individual cannot exist without the total. The wave has no existence apart from the ocean. The individual gross, subtle and causal bodies have no existence apart from the total gross, subtle and causal bodies respectively.

The concept of individuality exists only in the individual and not in the total. For the total, what we term as individual is the total itself! For the wave, its own individuality and the other waves exist. But for the ocean, all waves are but itself. We feel that we are a part of the Lord, but for Him, we exist in Him as Him. From His (total) standpoint, the individual's gross, subtle and causal bodies are Him alone.

For the individual, the totality is only an inferred logical assumption, but not an actual perceived experience. This is so because the individual's mind is finite, and therefore cannot conceive the Infinite. Therefore all saints confess their incapacity to describe the glories, virtues, extent and attributes of the infinite Lord.

In fact even the individuality of an individual is an assumed identity, an imagined concept (*jīvaḥ śabdaḥ tathā pare*) which when enquired into, gets falsified and melts away. What can be shown as a wave, distinguishing it from the ocean and its waters? What can we call the individual gross, subtle and causal body, apart from the total gross, subtle and causal bodies and the underlying principle of Existence–Consciousness?

Let us think of the air we breathe. Does the air that is inhaled, exhaled or held within belong to the individual? Can we claim any of the five elements as belonging to the individual? Then how can the body made up of these five elements be an individual? Hence it is clear that the individual gross, subtle and causal bodies are one with the total gross, subtle and causal bodies respectively.

But who am 'I', free from the conditioning of the three bodies? 'I' am the Witness–Consciousness (*pratyag-vijñāna*) that is aware of the three bodies and the three states. Similarly free from the total gross, subtle and causal conditioning, God/Truth is the pure Existence (*pūrṇa sat*) that gives existence to all. Just as the essence of the wave and ocean, free from its conditioning of names and forms is the one water alone, 'I' am, in essence, infinite, Consciousness–Existence Truth alone.

Hanumanji was asked about his relationship with Shri Rama. He said, "From the standpoint of the body, I am His servant; as an individual, I am a part of Him; but as the pure Self, we are one."

Deha-buḍḍhyā tu dāso'haṁ jīva-buddhyā tvad-aṁśakaḥ.
Ātma-buddhyā tvam-evāhaṁ iti me niścayā matiḥ.

* * *

Earlier it was said in verse 21 that the Truth/Self is non-dual, one without a second. Will not the very existence of the world, if it is a second entity, repudiate the non-duality of the Truth? Also how can the changing world arise from the changeless Truth? Will not the Truth have to change its changeless nature to become the changing world? If so, how then can It be called the Truth which implies freedom from change? These doubts get resolved with the following verse.

चिन्मात्रैकरसे विष्णौ ब्रह्मात्मैक्यस्वरूपके ।
भ्रमेणैव जगज्जातं रज्ज्वां सर्पभ्रमो यथा ॥ २४ ॥

cinmātraikarase viṣṇau brahmātmaikya-svarūpake |
bhrameṇaiva jagaj-jātaṁ rajjvāṁ
sarpa-bhramo yathā || 24 ||

24. यथा = Just as; सर्पभ्रमः = (there arises) the delusion of the snake; रज्ज्वाम् = on the rope; भ्रमेण एव = owing to delusion alone (so too); जगत् = the world; जातम् = has arisen; चित्-मात्र-एक-रसे = in the homogenous pure Consciousness; विष्णौ = in the all-pervading; ब्रह्म-आत्म-ऐक्य-स्वरूपके = in (that which is of) the nature of oneness between Truth and the Self.

24. *Just as there arises the delusion of the snake on the rope, so too, owing to delusion alone, has the world arisen in the homogenous pure Consciousness, which is all-pervading and of the nature of oneness between Truth and the Self.*

Vedanta declares that the world is created due to a delusion and is itself an illusion superimposed upon the Truth/Self, like the illusion of a snake seen on a rope. An illusion is caused when what is actually there (rope/Truth) is not seen and thereafter what is not there is superimposed (snake/world). Thus non-apprehension (*āvaraṇa śakti*) and mis-apprehension (*vikśepa śakti*) together create an illusion. If the actual was seen in the first place, the illusion would not have arisen.

Every illuṣion (*adhyāsa*) needs a substratum (*adhiṣṭhāna*) e.g. snake vision on the rope, blueness in the sky, the world on the Truth/Self. The substratum (rope/Truth) does not undergo any intrinsic change to appear as the illusion (snake/world). The substratum itself appears as the illusion. The illusion in no way affects the substratum even when seen over a long period of time or repeatedly by many people. The rope/Truth does not become poisonous nor polluted by the vision of the snake or the world from beginningless time. Even though we may say that there exists both the substratum and the illusion, there actually exists the substratum alone. The illusion is born of the ignorance in the mind of one who perceives it (*bhrama eva jagat jātam*). And that which is born of ignorance cannot be real. The knowledge of the substratum totally removes the illusion. The substratum cannot be known in parts, nor is the illusion removed in parts. We cannot say that the tail of the 'snake vision' has disappeared, but the other end still looks like the head of the snake! The realisation that the entire world is an illusion and that I am the infinite Truth and the substratum of the illusion happens simultaneously.

For the illusion of the snake vision to 'appear' on the rope the following special conditions must exist:

a) There must be a similarity (*sādṛśatvam*) between the substratum and the illusion e.g. both the rope and snake are long and slender.

b) There must exist an impression of the superimposed (an actual snake) in the one who sees the illusion (*satya sajātīya saṁskāra*).

c) There must be some emotions like attachment, fear etc. with respect to the superimposed in the one who sees the illusion (*pramātā doṣa*). Were it not for the fear, or strong emotions related to the snake, its superimposition would not have occured.

d) To see any illusion, there must be faulty vision in one who sees (*pramāṇa doṣa*). One with a keen vision would have seen the rope straight away.

e) There should also be the knowledge that the substratum exists (*sāmānya jñāna*), but not its exact nature. The person knows that something is, but does not know what it is and then superimposes the snake vision.

The illusion of the world is experienced because the Truth is beyond the perception of the senses and cognition of the mind. Due to that (non-apprehension), the world is projected. Also there exists in us impressions of the world from innumerable lifetimes wherein we have considered it real and developed strong likes, dislikes, attachments etc for it. We all know that 'I am' (*sāmānya jñāna*), but we do not know exactly who I am. We also know that the world 'exists', but do not know its true nature. The majority of us do not even have access to a valid means of knowledge (Vedantic knowledge taught by a qualified teacher). In its absence, the illusion continues unquestioned.

* * *

What do other schools of philosophy believe to be the relationship between the individual and the Truth/God? The next verse explains the fallacy in their belief and indicates the Vedantic standpoint.

तार्किकाणां तु जीवेशौ वाच्यावेतौ विदुर्बुधाः ।
लक्ष्यौ च साङ्ख्ययोगाभ्यां
वेदान्तैरैक्यता तयोः ॥ २५ ॥

tārkikāṇāṁ tu jīveśau vācyāvetau vidurbudhāḥ|
lakṣyau ca sāṅkhya-yogābhyāṁ
vedāntair-aikyatā tayoḥ || 25 ||

25. बुधाः = Wise people; विदुः = know (understand); एतौ = (that) these two; जीव-ईशौ = the individual and the Lord; वाच्या = in their literal meanings; तार्किकाणाम् तु = in the case of logicians; च = and; साङ्ख्य-योगाभ्याम् = in the case of *Sankhya* and *Yoga*; लक्ष्यौ = the implied meanings; ऐक्यता = the identity; तयोः = of both these; वेदान्तैः = by the Vedantins.

> 25. *Wise people know (understand) that the logicians accept only the literal meanings of the individual and the Lord/Truth, the Sankhya and Yoga the implied meanings, and the Vedantins the identity of both.*

The six main schools of philosophy who believe in the *Vedas* as the valid means of knowledge (*āstika darśana*) are *Nyāya* or *Tarka, Vaiśeṣika, Sāṁkhya, Yoga, Pūrva Mīmāṁsā* and *Uttara Mīmāṁsā* or *Vedānta.* Each understands the statement 'That thou art' (*Tat tvam asi*) which establishes the identity or relationship between the individual and the Truth/God, according to its belief.

Tārkikās or *Nayyāyikās* who follow the *Nyāya* school of philosophy are realists and believe only in that which can be proved by logic. They expound that the individual has the inherent qualities of joy, sorrow, desire etc. The Lord has the inherent quality of omniscience, omnipotence, overlordship etc. Consciousness is the individual's and the Lord's special quality. A thing can never lose its inherent quality and therefore the differences between the individual and the Lord are absolute (*atyanta bheda*). The individual loses his special quality of Consciousness in Liberation to become inert!

Those who follow the *Sāṁkhya* and *Yoga* schools of philosophy explain that both the individual and God are of the nature of Consciousness. However they are not one as God is omniscient, omnipotent and the individual is not. So even though they seem to go beyond the literal meaning (*vācyārtha*) towards the indicated meaning (*lakṣyārtha*), they only look at the individual and God with their conditioning, and therefore say that they are different.

For Vedantins the very purpose of human existence is to realise our identity with the infinite Truth/ Self. This is possible only when we go beyond the literal meaning to the indicative meaning of the words 'That thou art'. This is elaborated in the next verse.

Liberation to a Vedantin is not to attain the inertia of a stone as propounded by the logicians or to forever remain unattached from the inert as explained by the *Sāṁkhyans* or to remain in a thoughtless state as taught by the *Yogins*. Liberation for them is to sport in this world knowing it to be an illusion and realising oneself to be the infinite Self.

* * *

The very essence of Vedanta is the oneness between the individual and the Truth/God. This is here established with the analysis of the great sentence (*mahāvākya*) 'That thou art' (*tat tvam asi*).

कार्यकारणवाच्यांशौ जिवेशौ यौ जहच्च तौ ।
अजहच्च तयोर्लक्ष्यौ चिदंशावेकरूपिणौ ॥ २६ ॥

kārya-kāraṇa-vācyāṁśau jiveśau yau jahacca tau|
ajahacca tayor-lakṣyau cidaṁśāveka-rūpiṇau || 26||

26. यौ कार्य-कारण-वाच्य-अंशौ = That effect and cause aspects of the literal meaning; जिव-ईशौ = of the individual and the Lord/Truth; तौ = they both; जहत् च = are to be discarded; तयोः च = and those two; लक्ष्यौ = implied meanings; चित्-अंशौ = which is the Consciousness aspect; एकरूपिणौ = of the same nature; अजहत् = are not to be discarded.

26. The effect and cause aspects of the literal meaning of the individual and the Lord/Truth are to be discarded and the implied meaning which is the Consciousness aspect and of the same nature are not to be discarded.

The individual (*jīva*) knows himself to be Consciousness directly (*aparokṣatayā*) ('I know' I am and 'I know' the world exists). Wielding the finite body-mind equipment, he realises that he has little knowledge (*alpajña*), little strength (*alpa-śakti*), is one of the created beings (*kārya*) and incomplete (*apūrṇa*). However, God (*Īśvara*) is considered as someone far away (*parokṣa*), omniscient (*sarvajña*), omnipotent (*sarva-śaktimān*), the creator of the universe (*kāraṇa*) and infinite (*pūrṇa*). With this literal meaning the two can never be identical. That which is directly experienced within cannot be far away nor that which is finite be infinite. The wave can never be the ocean, even if it assumes the form of a mammoth tidal wave.

However, the individual is finite only when identified with his finite gross, subtle and causal conditioning. Free from these he is the pure infinite Consciousness alone. Similarly God too appears distant and with omniscience, omnipotence, the Creator etc. with respect to His total gross, subtle and causal conditioning. He is in essence the infinite Existence-Consciousness alone. Hence in essence they are one, just as the wave and the ocean are both water alone. This method is called *jahal-ajahal-lakṣaṇa* wherein the conditionings are discarded and the essential nature retained to establish the identity between the individual and God/Truth.

* * *

Will not Self-realisation take place if we follow the teaching of the other schools of philosophy and different branches of knowledge?

कर्मशास्त्रे कुतो ज्ञानं तर्के नैवास्ति निश्चयः ।
साङ्ख्ययोगौ द्विधापन्नौ
शाब्दिका शब्दतत्पराः ॥ २७ ॥

karma-śāstre kuto jñānaṁ tarke naivāsti niścayaḥ ।
sāṅkhya-yogau dvidhāpannau
śābdikā śabda-tatparāḥ ।। 27।।

27. कुतः = Where is; ज्ञानम् = knowledge; कर्म-शास्त्रे = in Scriptures dealing with rituals (*Mimāṁsā*); न एव अस्ति = there is certainly no; निश्चयः = firm conclusion; तर्के = in treatises on logic; द्विधा-आपन्नौ = duality is attained; साङ्ख्य-योगौ = in *Sankhya* and *Yoga* philosophies; शाब्दिकाः = the grammarians; शब्द-तत्-पराः = are intent only on words.

27. *Where is the possibility of knowledge in the Scriptures dealing with rituals (Mimāṁsā)? There is certainly no firm conclusion arrived at by the treatises on logic. Only duality is reached in Sāṅkhya and Yoga and the grammarians are intent only on words.*

***Karma-śāstre kuto jñānam* :** Those who believe in the Scriptures on rituals (*pūrva mimāṁsā*) say that only those statements of the *Vedas* which prompt man to action are meaningful. All others (that talk of knowledge) are futile (*āmnāyasya kriyārthatvāt, ānarthakyam atadarthānām*). Action cannot be the goal of life. Actions are meant to achieve some results. Results of finite actions, however elevating and subtle, are always finite. Hence to engage in difficult, time-consuming, exhausting and finite actions (rituals) cannot truly fulfil us. A mind that is pre-occupied with action is not available for subtle thoughts, research, meditation or knowledge, leave alone Self-realisation which is attained by the highest spiritual knowledge. The *Bhāgavatam* relates the story of the creator, Lord Brahma confessing that he was unable to teach Self-knowledge to his mind-born sons, the Sanat Kumaras, as his mind was too pre-occupied with work (*karmadhī*).

Tarke naivāsti niścayaḥ : The *Nayyāyikās* attempt prove their philosophy based on logic alone which they accept as the only means to knowledge. Logic is a double-edged sword. It can prove or disprove anything or nothing. Usually in a discussion, it is not the one who is right that wins, but one who has the stronger logic. The *Yoga Sūtras* therefore declare that 'logic cannot establish the Truth' (*tarko apratiṣṭhaḥ*). Intuitive knowledge is also beyond logic. Many who do not understand this, call it illogical. In Self-realisation, logic in line with the Vedantic thought is used to resolve the doubts that are obstacles in

Realisation. Also the intellect is used to its limit to realise its limitation in knowing the Truth. Einstein said, "There where science and logic ends, philosophy and religion begin." Swami Vivekananda, an intellectual, surrendered to Shri Ramakrishna whose spiritual state and behaviour was totally beyond his logic and reasoning.

Sāṁkhya–yogau dvidhāpannau : *Sāṁkhya* philosophy expounds that *Prakṛti*—the infinite power behind creation, is inert, eternal and real. *Puruṣa*—the Conscious Principle, which exists in the individual, as the governed and in the Lord, as the Governor is also eternal and real. Thus they establish two entities (duality)—*Prakṛti* and *Puruṣa*—of equal reality. This naturally limits both. Knowledge of a finite self cannot liberate us.

Śābdikā śabdatatparāḥ : Grammarians (*Vyyāyikās/śābdikās*) feel that the knowledge of grammar alone is the be all and end all of all fields of knowledge. Grammar (*vyākaraṇa*) is an ancilliary *Veda* (*vedāṅga*), which is studied to gain a better understanding of the *Vedas*. By no means can grammar be an independent means to realise the Truth/Self. The Truth indicated by the statements of the *Vedas* cannot be realised by merely understanding the sentence syntax, etymology of various words, their different meanings and grammar rules.

Adi Shankaracharya himself says in the renouned *Bhaja Govindam, "Na hi nahi rakṣati ḍukṛnj-karaṇe"*—grammar rules cannot protect you (from the jaws of death). Shri Chaitanya Mahaprabhu was one of the most brilliant grammarians of his time. When love for the Lord (*bhakti*) filled his heart, he realised the futility of his scholarship and gave up his professorship to sing the glories of the Lord.

* * *

What is the place of the other schools of philosophy who do not accept the *Vedas* as the valid means of knowledge?

अन्ये पाखण्डिनः सर्वे ज्ञानवार्तासुदुर्बलाः ।
एकं वेदान्तविज्ञानं स्वानुभूत्या विराजते ॥ २८ ॥

anye pākhaṇḍinaḥ sarve jñāna-vārtāsu-durbalāḥ |
ekaṁ vedānta-vijñānaṁ svānubhūtyā virājate || 28 ||

28. अन्ये सर्वे = All others; पाखण्डिनः = the heretics; ज्ञान-वार्तासु दुर्बलाः = are weak in Self-knowledge; एकम् = the one; वेदान्त-विज्ञानम् = wisdom of Vedanta; स्वानुभूत्या = because of its direct experience; विराजते = shines forth brilliantly.

28. All other heretics are weak in Self-knowledge. The one wisdom of Vedanta, because of its direct experience, shines forth brilliantly.

The three other main schools of thought that are an off-shoot of the Hindu Dharma are the Chārvāk, Jainism and Buddhism. In more recent times, the Sikhism also have emerged as a sect of Hindu Dharma.

The Chārvāks accept direct perception (*pratyakṣa pramāṇa*) as the only means to knowledge. Since space is not perceived by any of the five sense organs of perception, they say it is not an element like earth, water, fire or air. The hereafter is unseen, the soul unknown. Hence they maintain that to eat, drink and be merry is the goal of existence. The talk of Self-realisation does not arise for them. Many, knowingly or unknowingly believe in this philosophy.

The Jain sect arose in the later Vedic period and was revitalised by Vardhamana Mahavira in sixth century B.C.

The Jains believe that *dharma*, *adharma*, time, space, matter and *jīva* are eternal and imperishable entities. The *ātmā* is a live entity and all things have an *ātmā*. Liberation is a special condition of the *ātma* which is free of all pain and in which one remains eternally. One attains Liberation by the exhaustion of *karmas*.

Some Buddhists believe the Truth to be a void (*śūnya*) from which everything emerges and merges moment to moment (*kṣaṇika vijñāna vāda*).

The Vedantins refute the above with the following arguments.

a) If 'void' is an unknown entity, one cannot talk of it. If known, its knower is surely a conscious and existing entity. That Consciousness–Existence that knows the presence and absence of things is the infinite Truth/Self.

b) The direct experience (*aparokṣānubhūti*) of innumerable sages through the ages of the infinite Truth as being pure Consciousness and one with the Self cannot be ignored.

The Sikhs today consider themselves a separate sect different from Hindus. However, their philosophy, culture, rituals and spiritual practices are essentially the same as that of the Hindus.

Shaivism, Vaishnavism etc. are sects of the Hindu Dharma. Jainism, Buddhism and Sikhism too have emerged from the Hindu Dharma alone.

Jainism and Buddhism believe in the law of *karma*, rebirth, heaven and hell, a moral code of conduct, many spiritual practices and rituals similar to those of the Hindus, and even a similar life style (in India). They too do not believe in eternal hell or damnation. However, they do not accept the *Vedas* as the valid means of knowledge. This makes their stance, as far as Self-knowledge is concerned, weak.

In and before the time of Adi Shankaracharya (8th Century A.D.), philosophic debates and competitions (*śāstrārtha*) were common. (In this day and age of reconciliation and pseudo-secularism, it is considered unfashionable, fanatic and a waste of time to reveal the defects in another's philosophy. In fact many take pains to highlight the commonality, because they either do not have a clear conviction about any particular school of thought, want to avoid conflict, or have not gone deep into anything). During the debate, the one who was defeated, joined the winner's school of thought. During Adi Shankaracharya's time there existed hundreds of sects, prominent amongst whom were the ones mentioned in this text, who engaged in endless argumentations and rhetorics. Adi Shankaracharya, a spiritual giant of his time, refuted all such sects, convincing their prominent heads of his wisdom and bringing them under the fold of the holistic and undisputed Vedantic philosophy and true Hindu way of life.

On examination, the Vedantic philosophy is proved to be universal (applies to all mankind for all times), time-tested, most consistent, with an unbroken lineage of Teacher-taught (*paramparā*), intellectually subtle and logical, with the most exhaustive Scriptures and great luminaries like Adi

Shankaracharya, Swami Vivekananda, Ramana Maharshi, Swami Chinmayananda etc. expounding it. Good enough reasons to have full faith in it!

* * *

Without going into technicalities and different schools of philosophies, is there a simple way to understand the concepts of bondage and Liberation?

अहं ममेत्ययं बन्धो नाहं ममेति मुक्तता ।
बन्धमोक्षौ गुणैर्भाति गुणाः प्रकृतिसंभवाः ॥ २९ ॥

ahaṁ mametyayaṁ bandho nāhaṁ mameti muktatā|
bandhamokṣau guṇairbhāti guṇāḥ prakṛti-
sambhavāḥ || 29||

29. अयम् = This; बन्धः = bondage; अहम् मम इति = is of the nature of 'I' and 'my'; न इति = the negation; अहम् मम = of 'I' and 'my'; मुक्तता = is Liberation; बन्ध-मोक्षौ = bondage and Liberation; भाति = appear; गुणैः = because of the *gunas;* गुणाः = the *gunas;* प्रकृति-संभवाः = are born of *Prakṛti.*

29. This bondage is of the nature of 'I' and 'my'. The negation of 'I' and 'my' is Liberation. Bondage and liberation appear because of the gunas and the gunas *are born of Prakṛti.*

The notion of 'I' (*aham*) in what I am not, is the root of all sorrow. Things or people related to 'I', we refer to as 'my' (*mama*)—my house, my spouse etc. Towards such things and beings, we feel possessive, are attached, fear their loss, work to sustain them, strive to maintain relationships, and rejoice and suffer with them and because of them. The 'my'ness strengthens the false notion of 'I' and vice versa, as for example in the case of attachment to my children which deepens the thoughts that 'I am the body' and viceversa. To remove the false 'I' notion is relatively difficult. By removing all its supports of 'my' ness, the false 'I' notion weakens and is then easier to negate. We are therefore advised to—

a) Consider everything as God's.

b) Share all that is 'mine' with others.

c) Realize that 'my'ness causes sorrow and develop dispassion.

d) Understand that 'my'ness is only in our mind and not in any object or being, and is hence a purely subjective notion, subject to change according to external circumstances and moods of the mind. It is therefore not real or absolute.

e) Understand that things and beings come and go according to the results of our actions (*prārabdha*), and are with us only for a short time for us to enjoy or suffer. We should therefore not either hold on to or reject them, but make the best use of them for our own and others' welfare. Khalil Gibran in 'The Prophet' says, "Your children are not your children. They come through you but not from you. And though they are with you, yet they belong not to you." "Love one another, but make not a bond of love."

Māyā/Prakṛti, the infinite creative power of God has three inherent qualities—*sāttva, rajas* and *tamas*. Hence everything in the creation has these in different permutation and combinations. These qualities are not matter nor are they the content of matter, but their effects manifest in matter (*kāryānumeyā*). The main characteristic of *sattvaguṇa* is knowledge and that of *rajas* is activity. *Tamas* obstructs both knowledge and action and is characterised by inertia.

Our body and more importantly our mind has these three qualities, which become a part of our nature and bind us. *Sattva* binds us with joy (born of higher forms of knowledge, art etc.), *rajas* with a compulsive drive for action and *tamas* by veiling our knowledge (*Sattvam sukhe sañjayati, rajo karmaṇi bhārata, jñānam āvṛtya tu tamaḥ*—the *Geeta*). Goodness and compassion (*sātvic* qualities) also make us grieve at the sorrow of others. The sorrow that results from selfishness (*rājasic* quality) or laziness (*tāmasic* quality) are well-experienced.

However *sattva* being enobling, subtle and purifying, has the ability to liberate us, whereas *rajas* and *tamas* being agitating, obstructive and destructive, only lead us to bondage and sorrow. We are therefore advised to increase *sattvaguṇa* by making all our actions *sātvic*. Finally in a very highly *sātvic* mind, Self-realisation takes place which once and for all removes the false notion of 'I' in the body and 'my'-ness in things related to it.

* * *

The author laments the condition of those who, even while seeing, see not the Truth/Self.

ज्ञानमेकं सदा भाति सर्वावस्थासु निर्मलम् ।
मन्दभाग्या न जानन्ति स्वरूपं
केवलं बृहत् ॥ ३० ॥

jñānamekaṁ sadā bhāti sarvāvasthāsu nirmalam |
mandabhāgyā na jānanti svarūpaṁ
kevalaṁ bṛhat || *30* ||

30. एकम् = The one; निर्मलम् = pure; ज्ञानम् = Knowledge; सदा = always; भाति = shines; सर्व-अवस्थासु = in all the states of experiences; मन्द-भाग्याः = the unfortunate; न जानन्ति = are not aware; स्वरूपम् = their nature; केवलम् = homogenous; बृहत् = infinite.

30. *The One Pure Knowledge always shines in all the states of experiences. The unfortunate are not aware of their real nature which is homogenous and infinite.*

We are considered unfortunate if we miss out on the main attraction in a tourist spot. It would be like spending hard-earned money and time to go all the way to the Niagara and only use the swimming pool of the hotel and return without seeing the falls! We have earned this human birth with a lot of effort (*baḍe bhāga mānuṣa tanu pāyā*). To depart without knowing the Truth/Self that stares at us everywhere, all the time, and in every situation and condition is indeed unfortunate and a great loss (*na ced iha avedit mahati vinaṣṭiḥ—Īśāvasya Upaniṣad*).

Not all of us can hope to travel to a space station like Dennis Tito did. He had the money and health to do so and thus became the first commercial passenger to space in 2001, on flight X-37 White Knight. If we had to search for or attain the Truth/Self with money in some remote place, or with special equipment, only a few would be qualified to know It. But the Truth/Self is available to all, in every experience of life.

"The wise, with the eye of Wisdom, see the Truth in all experiences, whereas the deluded do not."

Utkrāmantaṁ sthitaṁ vāpi bhuñjānaṁ vā guṇānvitam
Vimūḍhā nānupaśyanti, paśyanti jñāna-cakṣuṣā.
- The *Geeta*.

We are so fascinated with the story, screenplay etc. that we fail to notice the spotless screen on which the characters of the movie play around.

The *Bhāgavatam* predicted that the people of our times (*Kali Yuga*) would indeed be lazy, intellectually dull, unfortunate and agitated and therefore would be unable to live happily (*mandāḥ sumanda-matayaḥ, manda-bhāgyāḥ hyupaddhṛtāḥ*).

* * *

It was said in verse 21 that 'I am Pure Knowledge'. Is not knowledge normally understood as information, as in words and thoughts available in books, on the internet or in the minds of people? This doubt is clarified as follows.

सङ्कल्पसाक्षि यज्ज्ञानं सर्वलोकैकजीवनम् ।
तदेवास्मीति यो वेद स मुक्तो नात्र संशयः ॥ ३१ ॥

saṅkalpa-sākṣi yajjñānaṁ sarvalokaika-jīvanam |
tadevāsmīti yo veda sa mukto nātra saṁśayaḥ || *31* ||

31. यत् ज्ञानम् = That Knowledge; सङ्कल्प-साक्षि = which is the Witness of all thoughts; सर्व-लोक-एक-जीवनम् = (and) the one Life Principle of all beings; यः = one

who; वेद = knows; इति = thus; तत् एव अस्मि = 'That alone I am'; सः = he; मुक्तः = is Liberated; न = there is no; संशयः = doubt; अत्र = in this matter.

31. *One who knows that Knowledge which is the Witness of all thoughts, and the one Life Principle of all beings as "That alone I am," he alone is Liberated. There is no doubt in this matter.*

Knowledge as information is available as words and thoughts. Such knowledge always has an 'object of knowledge' e.g. knowledge of history, science etc. That Awareness because of which we know such knowledge is called 'Pure Knowledge'. Awareness is always experienced within as 'I' and cannot become an object of knowledge. E.g. 'I know' history, science etc. Awareness is the Witness of all the knowledge available as thoughts and words.

Light is the manifestation of electricity in the bulb through the medium of the filament. The one and the same electricity can be called the light/life of all lighted bulbs. Similarly life is the manifestation of pure Knowledge (Awareness or Consciousness) in the gross body through the medium of the subtle body. Hence Consciousness manifests as the very life of all beings. Living beings (*jīvas*) are many, but the life in them (*jīvana*) is one.

The vital airs (*prāṇās*) support life in the body. Consciousness is the very support of the vital airs (*prāṇasya prāṇaḥ*). Air, water and food support life in the body but are not life-givers or life itself. When life no longer manifests in the body, life-supports, whether natural or man-made have no role to play. Life is holy as it is His divine expression. The body devoid of life is considered inauspicious and cremated or buried. Scientists despite advanced technology are unable to create new life or species. A clone is made from a living cell of another being. It is God/the Self alone who is the Creator of countless living beings, exists in them as life, and both gives and supports life. The Hindus therefore worship 'life'—be it in plants, animals or human beings. In the beginning of creation when the Lord decided to sport, He thought, "May I produce many living beings" (*bahusyāṁ prajāyeyeti*). Knowing that 'I' am the life in all, how can I hurt or kill another being? The *Bhāgavatam* says that even whilst carrying the king in a palanquin, Rishabhadeva kept jumping about to avoid trampling on insects and ants as they passed through the forest. Life is indeed one of His divine glories (*jīvanaṁ sarva bhūteṣu*) without which this universe would be bare and lifeless (literally and figuratively)!

* * *

What are the constituents of all our experiences? Awareness illumines all experiences. Then what illumines Awareness? These questions are answered hereafter.

प्रमाता च प्रमाणं च प्रमेयं प्रमितिस्तथा ।
यस्य भासावभासन्ते मानं ज्ञानाय तस्य किम् ॥ ३२ ॥

pramātā ca pramāṇaṁ ca prameyaṁ pramitistathā |
yasya bhāsāvabhāsante mānaṁ jñānāya tasya kim || 32||

32. प्रमाता = The knower; च = and; प्रमाणम् = the means of knowledge; च = and; प्रमेयम् = the object of knowledge; तथा = and; प्रमितिः = the knowledge of an object; यस्य = by whose; भासा = effulgence; अवभासन्ते = they are (all) illuminated; ज्ञानाय = for the knowledge; तस्य = of that; किम् = what is the need; मानम् = for a means of Knowledge.

32. *By whose effulgence the knower, the means of knowledge, the object of knowledge, the knowledge of an object are (all) illumined, for knowing That (Knowledge), what is the need for a means of knowledge?*

No experience or knowledge is possible without the following:

1. The object of knowledge (*prameya*): This may be a gross, inert, external object like the book you hold and read, or a person or abstract or

subtle ideas like the subject you are trying to understand—Vedanta.

2. The means of knowledge (*pramāṇa*): The three main means are direct perception (*pratyakṣa pramāṇa*), inference (*anumāna pramāṇa*) and the spoken or written word (*śabda pramāṇa*). Eg. The hands that hold the book, the eyes that read the words and the words that convey the knowledge.

3. The knower of the knowledge (*pramātā*): 'I', the individual (*jīva*) is the one who knows. Individuality is endowed with the reflection of Consciousness (*cidābhāsa*) that enables it to know. E.g. 'I know' that this is a book I hold, read and understand.

4. The knowledge or experience itself (*pramiti*): This exists as an illumined thought modification (*vṛtti jñāna*) as a result of the alignment of the *prameya, pramāṇa* and *pramātā*. E.g. "I hold and read this book, and understand its contents."

5. The illuminator of the above (*caitanya/bhāsa jñāna*): The entire experience happens in the presence of Consciousness, which reflects in the thought as *cidābhāsa*. Eg. even if I have a good eyesight and a book in front of me in a

language I understand, I can read only if I am alive.

How does Consciousness get illumined? Is there another Consciousness that illumines it? Consciousness is self-shining and self-evident. There is no other consciousness to illumine it, nor is it required. Does the sun need the light of a lamp to illumine it? It is by the light of the sun alone that all on earth is illumined. Similarly it is in the light of Consciousness alone that all else is known (*tasya bhāsā sarvam idaṁ vibhāti*). No other entity is needed to illumine It—and anyway no other entity really exists other than this One Supreme Consciousness!

* * *

The process of knowledge is now explained:

अर्थाकारा भवेद्वृत्तिः फलेनार्थ प्रकाशते ।
अर्थज्ञानं विजानाति स एवार्थः परः स्मृतः ॥ ३३ ॥

arthākārā bhavedvṛttiḥ phalenārtha prakāśate।
arthajñānaṁ vijānāti sa evārthaḥ paraḥ smṛtaḥ ।। 33।।

33. वृत्तिः = The thought; भवेत् = takes; अर्थ-आकाराः = the form of the object; अर्थः = the object; प्रकाशते = is illumined; फलेन = by the reflected Consciousness; विजानाति = (that which) knows; अर्थ-ज्ञानम् = the knowledge of the object; सः = that; एव = alone; परः अर्थः = Supreme Self; स्मृतः = is known.

33. The thought takes the form of the object. The object is illumined by the reflected Consciousness. That which has the knowledge of the object, is known (by the wise) as the Supreme Self.

The word *artha* has many meanings. In words like *puruṣārtha* it means effort (put in by man) or 'goal'—that which is sought after (by man). With the same meaning *svārtha* means striving only for oneself (selfish), *parārtha* is to strive for others and *paramārtha* is to seek or strive for the Supreme. Here the word *artha* is used to mean an object of knowledge and *paraḥ arthaḥ* as the Supreme (Self).

When an object (*artha*), say this book (*pustaka*), is in front of our eyes, and we are reading or at least seeing the book attentively, then a thought modification of the form of the words or book (*śabdākāra vṛtti* or *pustakākāra vṛtti*) takes place. The thought modification in the form of the object (*arthākāra vṛtti*) removes the ignorance of that object. This in turn is illumined by the individual endowed wich the reflection of Consciousness (*cidābhāsa*) called *pramātā* in the previous verse. This enables us to 'know' the object (words or book) which by themselves are inert.

Buddhitatstha-cidābhāsau dvāvapi vyāpnuto pustakam. Tatrājñānaṁ dhiyā naśyed ābhāsena pustakam sphuret.—Pañcadaśī : 7.91

However no reflection is possible without a reflecting medium. The thought modification (*vṛtti*) acts like the reflecting medium in which the individual, endowed with the reflection of Consciousness, reflects. Also how can there be a reflection without that which is reflected. It is the Pure Consciousness or the Supreme Self alone which is manifest in the thought as the reflection of Consciousness because of which every knowledge is possible. Every thought or experience is thus illumined directly by Consciousness (*sāmānya jñāna*), as is every other object in the world, and also by its special manifestation (*viśeṣa jñāna*) as the reflection of the Consciousness (*cidābhāsa*). E.g. A reflection creates a spot light on a wall exposed to sunlight. The spot light shows us minute cracks on the wall. The cracks are thus illumined directly by the sunlight and also by the reflected sunlight.

* * *

The difference in knowing other objects and the Truth/Self is now explained:

वृत्तिव्याप्यत्वमेवास्तु फलव्याप्तिः कथं भवेत्।
स्वप्रकाशस्वरूपत्वात् सिद्धत्वाच्च चिदात्मनः॥ ३४॥

vṛttivyāpyatvam-evāstu phalavyāptiḥ kathaṁ bhavet|
svaprakāśa-svarūpatvāt siddhatvācca cidātmanaḥ || 34||

34. चिदात्मनः = Of the Self which is of the nature of Consciousness; स्व-प्रकाश-स्वरूपत्वात् = because of the self-effulgent nature; च = and; सिद्धत्वात् = because it is self-evident; अस्तु = there is; वृत्ति-व्याप्यत्वम् = thought pervasion; एव = alone; कथम् = how; भवेत् = can there be; फल-व्याप्तिः = pervasion by reflected Consciousness.

34. Since the Self which is of the nature of Consciousness is self-effulgent and self-evident, there can only be thought pervasion. How can there be pervasion by reflected Consciousness?

As explained in the previous verse, the knowledge of objects happens as though in two steps:

1. Ignorance of the object is removed by the thought modification assuming the form of the object. Eg. This is a pot (*ghaṭākāra vṛtti*).
2. The individual endowed with the reflection of Consciousness, illumines the thought modification. E.g. 'I know' this is a pot. Even as I know the pot, I remain different from it. When the next thought comes, I illumine that also objectively, without partiality or reservation.

In Self-knowledge:

1. Ignorance of the Truth/Self is of the nature of individuality endowed with the reflection of Consciousness (*jīva bhāvā*). It manifests as 'I am finite, limited, the body, the doer' etc. This veiling of the Self is destroyed by the thought modification 'I am the infinite Truth' (*brahmākāra vṛtti*). The knowledge in this case is not, 'this is the Infinite Truth', but it is, 'I am the Infinite Truth'.

The thought modification being finite cannot actually objectify the infinite Truth (like in the example of a pot). It only objectifies the conditioned Self. However since the conditioned Self is of the nature of the infinite Truth, the veiling or ignorance of its infinite nature is destroyed. The *brahmākāra vṛtti* can arise only in a pure and subtle intellect that has understood the import of the nature of the Truth. It cannot be attained by mere repetition.

Swami Akhandananda Maharaj was asked if he had realised the Truth. He replied, "How can the infinite Self be realized or become known? All I can say is that the veiling has been destroyed (*āvaraṇa bhaṅga huā hai*)."

2. ***Phala Vyāpti*:** Here the object of the thought and the knower/subject is the same.

There cannot therefore be a knower illumining the Self/Truth. Hence *phala vyāpti* is not possible. Also the thought (*brahmākāra vṛtti*) having achieved its purpose of destroying the veiling, disappears, and the Infinite Self alone remains. How can the *brahmākāra vṛtti,* which is inert, and a manifestation of ignorance, remain on the destruction of the veiling of ignorance (*ajñāna āvaraṇa*)? The effect surely disappears with the destruction of its cause.

Once the *brahmākāra vṛtti* disappears, there remains no medium of reflection for the *cidābhāsa* or the finite self (*jīva bhāvā*). There can be no reflection of the Sun in the bucket when the water has been poured out. The reflection, so to speak, merges into the Sun. Similarly the *cidābhāsa* merges into the Self (*cid*).

Then who illumines the Self? The Self is self-shining and self-evident. It needs nothing nor is there anything, which can illumine It. The reflection of Consciousness is its mere finite manifestation. How can it illumine Consciousness/Self, its infinite source? How can the reflection of the Sun illumine the Sun (*svayaṁ sphuraṇa-rūpatvāt na ābhāsa upayujyate*)?

* * *

Do the thoughts of the mind ever cease? Other than in sleep, can we ever go beyond the continuous flow of thoughts?

अर्थादर्थान्तरे वृत्तिर्गन्तुं चलति चान्तरे ।
निराधारा निर्विकारा या दशा सोन्मनी स्मृता ॥ ३५ ॥

arthād-arthāntare vṛttir-gantuṁ calati cāntare |
nirādhārā nirvikārā yā daśā sonmanī smṛtā || *35* ||

35. वृत्तिः = The thought; गन्तुम् = goes; अर्थात् = from one object; अर्थ-अन्तरे = to another object; चलति = moves; च अन्तरे = and in between; या = that; दशा = state (of the mind); निराधारा = which exists without any support; निर्विकारा = (and) without any modifications; सा = that (state); स्मृता = is known as; उन्मनी = *Unmani*.

35. Thoughts move from one object to another. And in between that state of the mind which exists without any support and without any modifications is known as Unmani.

The mind is a continuous flow of thought-modifications (*vṛttis*). A thought stays for a mere fraction of a second. The flow seems continuous because of the speed. Nature does not like voids. The thoughts are fueled and driven by our nature (*prakṛti*), or inherent tendencies (*vāsanās*), the ego (*ahaṁkāra*) or ignorance of the Self (*ajñāna*).

(*icchā dveṣa samutthena dvandva mohena bhārata*—The *Geeta*)

The ignorance of the Self, and the sense of individuality—the ego in all of us is the same, but our inherent tendencies differ. Hence, each one thinks in his/her own unique way. Also the innumerable objects of the world cause an innumerable variety of thoughts in different minds, and in the same mind also, at different times. *Sātvic* thoughts are steady and focussed, *rājasic* thoughts fast and distracted and *tāmasic* thoughts sluggish and dull.

However fast the thoughts, there does exist at least a minute gap between any two thoughts. One of the techniques in meditation (as described in verse 9) is to focus on this gap and attempt to lengthen the same. This finally results in the cessation of all thoughts. Another method is given in the *Māṇḍukya Kārikā* : 3.32—'When by the knowledge of the Truth/Self, thoughts cease, a state of 'no mind' is reached as there is no object left for the thought to objectify.'

(*ātmāsatyānubnodhena na saṁkalpayate yadā*
manasāṁ tadā yāti grahyābhave tadagraham)

This state is called *Unmani*—a state beyond the grasp of the mind. Such a state of Knowledge is difficult for an ordinary mind in ignorance to comprehend. Therefore, most dismiss such a state of the realised one as a trance or madness. Once the Truth/Self is realised, and one is firmly rooted in it, the presence or absence of thoughts do not affect the person. Such a state is called *Sahaja Samādhi.*

Great saints, when overwhelmed by the love of God, go into a state called *Bhāva Samādhi.* This was seen quite frequently in Shri Ramakrishna Paramahamsa and Chaitanya Mahaprabhu. Very few manage to understand even that. As for an ordinary person, only his or her state of agitation and distraction is normal, natural and real to him or her. It is strange indeed that while artificial means to quieten the mind like drinks are considered fashionable by many, any attempt at quietening the mind by meditation, devotion or knowledge is considered a waste of time or escapism. Whatever be it, only a realised person can truly fathom the state of Realisation. We can only guess at and imagine the Bliss he experiences.

* * *

We have heard of a coloured mind. What remains when it loses its colouring?

चित्तं चिच्च विजानीयात्तकाररहितं यदा ।
तकारो विषयाध्यासो जपारागो यथा मणौ ॥ ३६ ॥

cittaṁ cicca vijānīyāt-takārarahitaṁ yadā।
takāro viṣayādhyāso japārāgo yathā maṇau ।। 36।।

36. यदा = When; तकार-रहितम् = (the *Cit-ta*) is without the *ta*; विजानीयात् = know that; चित्तम् चित् च = the mind is itself the Consciousness. तकारः = The *ta*; विषय-अध्यासः = represents the superimposition of the objects; यथा = just as; मणौ = in the crystal; जपा-रागः = the colour of a china-rose (is superimposed).

> 36. *When the Cit-ta (mind) is without the* ta *know that the Citta (mind) is itself the Cit (Consciousness). The* ta *represents the superimposition of the objects just as in the crystal the colour of china-rose is superimposed.*

The definition given here is simple.

I/Consciousness (*cit*) + object (*ta*) = thought/ mind (*citta*).

Mind (*citta*)—object (*ta*) = Pure Consciousness (*cit*).

Likes and dislikes colour the mind (*rañjanāt rāgaḥ*). Also thoughts assume the form and quality of the things and emotions they objectify. By identifying with them we too become of that nature. E.g. I am happy, unhappy, angry etc.

The crystal by itself is colourless. It appears red or blue when red or blue cloth is kept in its proximity, but even at that time it is intrinsically colourless. Similarly, even when I identify with objects and thoughts, and appear of that nature, I am intrinsically the Pure Consciousness alone. When the thoughts of objects cease, the Pure Consciousness is experienced. Once as Shri Rama and Sita were sitting on a crystal boulder on the bank of the river at Chitrakuta, Jayanta, Indra's son came to test His divinity by assuming the form of the crow and hurting Sita. The crystal boulder reflected both the divine form and the sport of Shri Rama and Sita and also the ugly form of Jayanta and his cruel act. It retained neither, remaining ever pure and the same.

"O dear mind, why do you run deluded like a ghost, hither and thither? See the Infinite Truth and by giving up all attachments to thoughts and objects, be happy. When you thus give up your attachments, there will no more be any thought fluctuations."

Aho cittaṁ kathaṁ bhrātaḥ pradhāvasi piśācavat
Abhinnaṁ paśya cātmānaṁ rāgatyāgāt sukhī bhava
Rāga tyāgāt punaḥ cittaṁ ekānekaṁ na vidyate

Doing one's duties as an offering to God, living a simple life of self-control, being in tune with nature, the attitude of acceptance, the company of noble souls, spiritual practices etc. help reduce our attachments to objects and thoughts and finally lead to Realisation.

* * *

Many in society call themselves, 'free and liberated'. We also hear of free trade, a country's freedom, freedom of the press, women's liberation etc. What is it to be truly and forever liberated?

ज्ञेयवस्तुपरित्यागात् ज्ञानं तिष्ठति केवलम् ।
त्रिपुटी क्षीणतामेति ब्रह्मनिर्वाणमृच्छति ॥ ३७ ॥

jñeyavastu-parityāgāt jñānaṁ tiṣṭhati kevalam |
tripuṭī kṣīṇatāmeti brahm-anirvāṇam-ṛcchati || *37*||

37. ज्ञानम् = Knowledge; केवलम् = alone; तिष्ठति = remains; ज्ञेय-वस्तु-परित्यागात् = out of the renunciation of the objects of knowledge; त्रिपुटी = the triad (of knower, knowledge and known); क्षीणताम् = cease; एति = attains; ऋच्छति = one reaches; ब्रह्म-निर्वाणम् = (the state of) Liberation.

37. Knowledge alone remains when the objects of knowledge are renounced. When the triad (of knower, knowledge and known), ceases, then one reaches the state of Liberation.

The three bodies spoken about earlier are categorised differently as the five sheaths (*pañca koṣāḥ*). The gross body is called the food sheath (*annamaya koṣa*), the subtle body is divided into the vital air sheath (*prāṇamaya koṣa*), mental sheath (*manomaya koṣa*) and intellectual sheath (*jñānamaya koṣa*); and the causal body is the Bliss sheath (*ānandamaya koṣa*).

Duality (*dvaita*) is experienced as the triads (*tripuṭi*) of the knower (*pramātā / jñātā*), the known (*prameya / jñeya*) and knowledge (*pramā / jñāna*). The 'knower' aspect of the individual endowed with the reflection of Consciousness (*jīva*) exists in the intellectual sheath (as knowledge is the function of the intellect). The known exists as the innumerable variety of sounds (*śabda*), sensations (*sparśa*), forms and colours (*rūpa*), tastes (*rasa*) and smells (*gandha*).

The knowledge exists as the illuminated thought modification (*artha jñānam*) (refer verse 33) in the mental sheath.

Vijñāna-maya utpanno jñātā jñānaṁ manomayaḥ
Jñeyaḥ śabdādayo naitat-trayam-utpattitaḥ pura— *Pañcadaśī* : 11.15

The known (*jñeya*) has no existence 'for us' except as thoughts (*jñāna*) in our mind. The thoughts have a momentary existence, each one pushing the previous one out of existence (*uttara kṣaṇa bādhita*). Knowledge is the result of an illusory relationship between the sentient knower and the inert known. The knower (ego) can only establish itself as an entity when there is something to be known and the resultant knowledge in the form of thoughts. E.g. 'I know, I am a man' or 'I know, this is a rose'. This individuality as a knower is the mere superimposition and an assumed entity which disappears when enquired into (*svayaṁ virūpaḥ svavicāra kāle dhāvati*). Hence the triad (*tripuṭi*) is interdependent and illusory. Knowing thus, man gets liberated from its hold.

To do anything one likes to do at any time is not freedom but rather only a sign of our bondage or slavery to our own mind. "To be able to say 'no' to our mind is to be free and truly liberated."—Pujya Gurudev Swami Chinmayananda. Most of us are compulsive thinkers, we have not the ability to start, stop or direct our thoughts at will. We are persecuted by our thoughts and get carried away by them. One thought leads to another through past association and often without any rhyme or reason. Thus we may boast that we are free or liberated because we do not follow traditions or the norms of society, but we are slaves of the whims and fancies of the mind. True freedom is to be the master of our mind.

In meditation, we attempt to make the mind free of objects. Thus thoughts cease and the pure Consciousness alone remains. Also by consciously not associating one thought with another, thoughts lose their momentum and cease. Once the triad ends, man is liberated once and forever. This is called the state of *Brahman*-hood (*brāhmī sthiti*) or *Nirvāṇa*.

* * *

The triad of the knower, known and knowledge, ends thus:

मनोमात्रमिदं सर्वं तन्मनो ज्ञानमात्रकम्।
अज्ञानं भ्रम इत्याहुर्विज्ञानं परमं पदम्॥ ३८॥

manomātramidaṁ sarvaṁ tanmano jñānamātrakam |
ajñānaṁ bhrama ityāhur-vijñānaṁ
paramaṁ padam || *38* ||

38. सर्वम् = All; इदम् = this; मनोमात्रम् = is nothing but the mind; तत्-मनः = that mind; ज्ञान-मात्रकम् = is of the nature of Knowledge; अज्ञानम् = ignorance; इति आहुः = is called (by the wise) as; भ्रमः = illusion; विज्ञानम् = *Vijñānam*; परमम् = supreme; पदम् = state.

> *38. All this is nothing but the mind. That mind is of the nature of Knowledge. Ignorance is called illusion by the wise and* Vijñāna *is the Supreme State.*

***Mano-mātram-idam sarvam*:** As mentioned in the previous verse, it is impossible to prove the existence of the world except as thoughts in our mind. The whole world exists for me only in my mind. This seems a staggering statement. 'Doesn't the world exist even when I am asleep?' True, but this too is known only when you wake up, and only as thoughts in your mind! 'But the world existed before I was born and will continue to do so even after I die!' Yes. This too is known to you, now, only as thoughts in your mind! 'But does not the world exist in the others' minds also?' Of course, but the concept of the other mind is also only in your mind! Strange that such fleeting illusory thoughts make the world appear so solid and real!

***Tatmano jñāna-mātrakam*:** What gives existence to thoughts? What endows them with the capacity to know? It is 'I' the pure Consciousness alone that gets reflected in the thoughts and lends them existence and awareness. There would be no thoughts or world without 'I'. Thus 'I' as the Pure Consciousness am the only Reality behind the thoughts and the world.

***Ajñāna-bhrama*:** Ignorance of the Self expresses as the finite individuality, the ego (*aham vṛtti*). Being a reflection, it, in reality, is the pure Self alone. Also, thoughts of ignorance like 'I am the body', 'I am mortal' etc. are opposed to thoughts of Knowledge like 'I am the infinite Truth'. For the Witness of the two, both are unreal. Also, can anyone really say, "I do not know myself?" Do we not experience ourselves, every moment and in every experience? To think, 'I am ignorant' is itself a delusion. Also ignorance is not an entity that we can comprehend or transact with. It has no independent existence. How can we give any reality to such an entity and suffer due to it? But strangely enough, we can trace all our sorrows to ignorance of the Self!

Vijñānam paraṁ padam: Understanding Vedanta leaves us, as ignorant beings, with no legs (illusions) to stand on. We fall flat on our noses (ego), ground into the Supreme Reality.

* * *

The following verse explains the relationship between the individual, the Lord and the Truth, with respect to *māyā*.

अज्ञानं चान्यथा ज्ञानं मायामेतां वदन्ति ते ।
ईश्वरं मायिनं विद्यान्मायातीतं निरञ्जनम् ॥ ३९ ॥

ajñānaṁ cānyathā jñānaṁ māyāmetāṁ vadanti te|
īśvaraṁ māyinaṁ vidyān-māyātītaṁ nirañjanam || 39||

39. ते = They (wise); वदन्ति = declare; एताम् = these two; अज्ञानम् = ignorance (non-apprehension); च = and; अन्यथा-ज्ञानम् = misapprehension; मायाम् = as *māyā*; ईश्वरम् = the Lord; विद्यात् = is to be known; मायिनम् = as the wielder of *māyā*; माया-अतीतम् = (that which is) beyond *māyā*; निरञ्जनम् = immaculate.

39. The wise declare these two—non-apprehension and misapprehension to be māyā. The Lord is the wielder of māyā and that which is beyond māyā is the immaculate (Self).

In Hindu philosophy, the Lord with form (*Saguṇa Brahma* or *Īśvara*) is always accompanied by His consort (*Māyā*). Both are worshipped together. Lord Brahma shares His throne with Saraswati, Lakshmi is always serving the feet of Lord Vishnu and Parvati is literally the 'better half' of the body of Lord Shiva (as *Ardhanārīśvara*). Even the incarnations of the Lord are always remembered with their consorts. *Siyāvara Rāmacandra, Rādhā-Kṛṣṇa* etc. *Māyā* is the inherent infinite creative power of the Lord. He wields it without getting deluded by it. *Māyā* remains under His control (*Māyāpati*) and He sports with her at will (*krīḍā sādhanā*). In His presence, *Māyā* creates this world of things and beings (*Mayā adhyakṣeṇa prakṛti sūyate sacarācara*—The *Geeta*).

Māyā however enslaves the created beings (*māyā dāsa*) by her two powers. They are the veiling (*āvaraṇa śakti*), which veils the Truth, and the power of projection (*vikṣepa śakti*), which projects the false. This is referred to here as ignorance of the Self (*Ātmā*) or non-apprehension (*ajñāna*) and identification with the non-Self (*anātmā*) or misapprehension (*anyathā jñāna*). Ignorance, remaining the same, causes manifold misapprehensions like the superimposition of happiness on objects and beings (*sukha adhyāsa*), the lending of absolute reality to the world (*jagati satyatva buddhi*), duality of the individual and the Truth (*jīva-brahma bheda*), the feeling of finitude (*jīva-bhāva* or *alpatā*), desires for objects or beings (*kāma*), anger towards the obstacles in fulfilling desires (*krodha*), greed for more (*lobha*), sorrow at the loss of desired objects (*shoka*), attachment (*āsakti*), delusions (*moha*), fears (*bhaya*) etc. The list is indeed endless. In short, *māyā* is calamitous for the ignorant individual (*anarthakārī*).

But when we enquire into the nature of *māyā* from its own stand-point, we find that it is indescribable. Being of the nature of ignorance, it cannot be said to exist (*sat*), yet its effects are observed, so we cannot say it does not exist (*asat*). Existence and non-existence cannot co-exist, so it is indeed indescribable (*sat-asadbhyām anirvacanīyam*). It is hence referred to as *mithyā* which denotes that it is neither *sat* nor *asat*.

The infinite, nameless, formless and quality-less (*Nirguṇa Brahma*) is beyond *māyā* (*māyātītam*) and in it, there is no trace of *māyā*. Being one without a second, it alone exists as the pure Self (*Ātmā*).

To summarise, the individual is enslaved by *māyā*, the Lord is in control of *māyā* and the Truth is beyond *māyā*. The Scriptures advice us to surrender to the Lord Who shall then take us beyond *māyā* (*mām eva ye prapadyante māyām etāṁ taranti te*). The path of Knowledge leads us beyond *māyā* by enabling us to know and realise our true nature.

* * *

Nature invokes various feelings in us. It is awesome, and to some, fearsome as darkness, thunder, lightning, storm and rain. Even as we witness such wonderous sights, we can reflect on the Truth through the beautiful metaphor given in the following two verses.

सदानन्दे चिदाकाशे मायामेघस्तटिन्मनः ।
अहंता गर्जनं तत्र धारासारो हि यत्तमः ॥ ४० ॥
महामोहान्धकारेऽस्मिन्देवो वर्षति लीलया ।
तस्या वृष्टेर्विरामाय प्रबोधैकसमीरणः ॥ ४१ ॥

sadānande cidākāśe māyāmeghas-taṭinmanaḥ |
ahantā garjanaṁ tatra dhārāsāro hi yattamaḥ || 40 ||
mahāmohāndhakāre'smin-devo varṣati līlayā |
tasyā vṛṣṭervirāmāya prabodhaika-samīraṇaḥ || 41 ||

40. चित्-आकाशे = In the sky of Consciousness; सत्-आनन्दे = (which is of the nature of) Existence and Bliss; माया-मेघः = *māyā* is the cloud; मनः = (and) the mind; तटित् = (is) (akin to) lightning; तत्र = there (in the metaphor); अहंता = ego; गर्जनम् = is the thunder; हि = verily; धारासारः = the downpour; यत् तमः = is the darkness.

41. अस्मिन् = In this; महा-मोह-अन्धकारे = pitch darkness of deep delusion; देवः = the Lord (*Īśvara*); वर्षति = rains; लीलया = sportingly; विरामाय = for the cessation; तस्याः = of this; वृष्टेः = downpour;

प्रबोध = Self-realisation; एक = alone; समीरणः = (is) the wind (which disperses the clouds).

40. *In the sky of Consciousness which is of the nature of Existence and Bliss, māyā is the cloud, the mind the lightning, the ego the thunder and verily the downpour is inertia.*

41. *In this pitch darkness of deep delusion, the Lord rains sportingly. For the cessation of this downpour, Self-realisation alone is the wind which disperses the clouds.*

Space is infinite and pure. It accommodates everything, remaining unaffected by anything. Rain clouds gather and thicken and the sky darkens. When this happens at night, the sky becomes pitch dark, with all the stars and the moon hidden. Due to an imbalance in electric charges, lightning strikes and thunder crashes. A very high negative charge emerges from the cloud at the speed of light in a tunnel of air. It electrocutes anything it touches. It produces various sounds like rumbling, cracking, clapping etc., which are sometimes frightening. When the clouds are thick enough, they bring down torrential rains which drench everything and at times even cause floods.

Similarly, in the sky of infinite Conscious-Existence-Bliss are seen the clouds of *māyā* or ignorance. When they thicken, they appear to darken the infinite sky / Self, even though they are mere vapour / *vāsanās*. The mind manifests from these *vāsanās* with lightning speed and illumines all in its way. The power of the mind is tremendous and, at times, devastating. Arjuna says, "Indeed, the mind is restless, stormy and with inexhaustable strength. To control it is like trying to control a storm or typhoon." Like lightning, the mind too has its own special beauty. The ego rumbles and thunders from this cloud of ignorance with notions like 'I am the body', 'I am the doer', 'I am the enjoyer', 'I die', 'I shall be born again' etc. The qualities of *sattva* (noble), *rajas* (dynamic) and *tamas* (dull) also rain down from these clouds of ignorance, drenching all things and beings.

The infinite sky / Self is unopposed to and accommodates the clouds, lightning and rain with all its sound-and-light effects and yet remains completely unaffected by them all. It is ignorance-created delusions alone that prevent us from experiencing the infinite Consciousness within. One strong gust of the breeze of Self-realisation is enough to scatter these menacing clouds of ignorance and *vāsanās*, and with them disperse the lightning, thunder and rain, leaving us to experience the breath-taking infinite Bliss within.

* * *

The following seven verses give various connotations of the words *jñānam* and *vijñānam* thereby defining different concepts and indicating methods of contemplation on the Truth and the meaning of 'Realisation'.

ज्ञानं दृग्दृश्ययोर्भानं विज्ञानं दृश्यशून्यता ।
एकमेवाद्वयं ब्रह्म नेह नानाऽस्ति किञ्चन ॥ ४२ ॥

क्षेत्रक्षेत्रज्ञयोर्ज्ञानं तज्ज्ञानं ज्ञनमुच्यते ।
विज्ञानं चोभयोरैक्यं क्षेत्रज्ञपरमात्मनोः ॥ ४३ ॥

परोक्षं शास्त्रजं ज्ञानं विज्ञानं चात्मदर्शनम् ।
आत्मनो ब्रह्मणः सम्यगुपाधिद्वयवर्जितम् ॥ ४४ ॥

त्वमर्थविषयं ज्ञानं विज्ञानं तत्पदाश्रयम् ।
पदयोरैक्यबोधस्तु ज्ञानविज्ञानसंज्ञितम् ॥ ४५ ॥

आत्मानात्मविवेकं च ज्ञानमाहुर्मनीषिणः ।
अज्ञानं चान्यथा लोके विज्ञानं तन्मयं जगत् ॥ ४६ ॥

अन्वयव्यतिरेकाभ्यां सर्वत्रैकं प्रपश्यति ।
यत्तु वृत्तिजं ज्ञानं विज्ञानं ज्ञानमात्रकम् ॥ ४७ ॥

अज्ञानध्वंसकं ज्ञानं विज्ञानं चोभयात्मकम् ।
ज्ञानविज्ञाननिष्ठेयं तत्सद्ब्रह्मणि चार्पणम् ॥ ४८ ॥

jñānaṁ dṛgdṛśyayor-bhānaṁ vijñānaṁ dṛśya-śūnyatā |
ekamevādvayaṁ brahma neha nānā'sti kiñcana || 42 ||

kṣetrakṣetrajñayor-jñānaṁ tajjñānaṁ jñanam-ucyate |
vijñānaṁ cobhayoraikyaṁ kṣetrajña-paramātmanoḥ || 43 ||

parokṣaṁ śāstrajaṁ jñānaṁ vijñānaṁ cātma-darśanam |
ātmano brahmaṇaḥ samyag-upādhi-dvaya-varjitam || 44 ||

tvam-artha-viṣayaṁ jñānaṁ vijñānaṁ
tat-padāśrayam |
padayoraikya-bodhastu jñāna-vijñāna-sañjñitam || 45 ||

ātmānātma-vivekaṁ ca jñānam-āhur-manīṣiṇaḥ |
ajñānaṁ cānyathā loke vijñānaṁ tanmayaṁ jagat || 46 ||

anvaya-vyatirekābhyāṁ sarvatraikaṁ prapaśyati |
yattu vṛttijaṁ jñānaṁ vijñānaṁ jñāna-mātrakam || 47 ||

ajñāna-dhvaṁsakaṁ jñānaṁ vijñānaṁ
cobhayātmakam |
jñānavijñāna-niṣṭheyaṁ tatsad-brahmaṇi
cārpaṇam || 48 ||

42. ज्ञानम् = Knowledge; भानम् = (is the) awareness; दृग्-दृश्ययोः = of (the distinction between) the Seer and the seen; विज्ञानम् = *Vijñānam*; दृश्य-शून्यता = (is the) absence of the seen (objects); ब्रह्म = Truth; एकम् एव अद्वयम् = is one and verily non-dual; इह = here; न अस्ति = there is no; नाना = multiplicity; किञ्चन = whatsoever.

43. तत्-ज्ञानम् = That knowledge; ज्ञनम् उच्यते = is called *Jñānam*; ज्ञानम् = which is the knowledge; क्षेत्र-क्षेत्रज्ञयोः = of the experienced and Experiencer; च = and; विज्ञानम् = *Vijñānam* (direct Realisation); ऐक्यम् = of the identity; उभयोः = of both; क्षेत्रज्ञ-परमात्मनोः = the Experiencer and the Supreme Lord/Self.

44. ज्ञानम् = *Jñānam;* परोक्षम् = (is) indirect; शास्त्रजम् = (when) born from the study of the Scriptures; च = and; विज्ञानम् = *Vijñānam;* आत्मदर्शनम् = self-Realisation; आत्मनः = of the Self; ब्रह्मणः = of the Truth; सम्यक्-उपाधि-द्वय-वर्जितम् = (is of the nature of) the total removal of the two types of conditionings.

45. ज्ञानम् = *Jñānam;* त्वम्-अर्थ-विषयम् = (is understanding) the essence of 'Thou'; विज्ञानम् = *Vijñānam;* तत्-पद-आश्रयम् = (is the knowledge) of the word 'That'; तु = verily; ऐक्य-बोधः = the Knowledge of the identity; पदयोः = between the two words; ज्ञान-विज्ञान-संज्ञितम् = (is) called *Jñāna-Vijñāna.*

46. च = And; मनीषिणः = the wise; आहुः = call; आत्म-अनात्म-विवेकम् = the discrimination between the Self and the not-Self; ज्ञानम् = *Jñānam;* च = and; लोक = in this world; अज्ञानम् = ignorance; अन्यथा = is to perceive differently (not-Self as Self); विज्ञानम् = *Vijñānam;* जगत् = (is to perceive) the world; तन्मयम् = as pervaded by Consciousness/Self.

47. प्रपश्यति = One comes to see clearly; एकम् = the one (Truth); सर्वत्र = everywhere; अन्वय-व्यतिरेकाभ्याम् = by the method of invariable concomittance; तु = further; यत् = that which; वृत्तिजम् = is born of thoughts; ज्ञानम् = (is called) *Jñānam;* विज्ञानम् = *Vijñānam;* ज्ञान-मात्रकम् = (is) Pure Knowledge (free from thoughts).

48. ज्ञानम् = *Jñānam;* अज्ञान-ध्वंसकम् = is the destroyer of ignorance; च = and; विज्ञानम् = *Vijñānam;* उभयात्मकम् = (is) of the nature of both; इयम् = this is; ज्ञान-विज्ञान-निष्ठा = abidance in *Jñāna* & *Vijñāna;* च अर्पणम् = which is the merging; तत्-सत्-ब्रह्मणि = in that ever-existing Truth.

42. *Jñānam is the awareness of the distinction between the Seer and the seen. Vijñānam is the absence of the seen (objects). The Truth is one and verily non-dual in which there is not multiplicity whatsoever.*

43. *That is called Jñānam which is the knowledge of the experienced and Experiencer. Vijñānam is the realisation of the identity of both the Experiencer and the Supreme Lord/Self.*

44. *Jñānam is indirect knowledge born from the study of the Scriptures. Vijñānam is self-Realisation of the nature of the total discarding of the two types of conditionings pertaining to the Self and the Truth.*

45. *Jñāna is understanding the essence of 'Thou' (in the statement 'That Thou Art'). Vijñāna is the knowledge of the word 'That'. Verily the knowledge of the identity between the two words is called Jñāna-Vijñāna.*

46. *The wise call the discrimination between the Self and the not-Self Jñāna. And in this world ignorance is to perceive differently (not-Self as Self). Vijñāna is to perceive the world as pervaded by Consciousness/the Self.*

47. *One comes to see clearly the one Truth everywhere by the method of invariable concomittance. Further that which is born of thoughts is called Jñāna. Vijñāna is Pure Knowledge (free from thoughts).*

48. *Jñāna is the destroyer of ignorance while Vijñāna is of the nature of both. Abidance in Jñāna & Vijñāna, is the merging in that ever-existing Truth.*

In different context, various meanings of the words *jñāna* and *vijñāna* are used in our Scriptures. Here are some of them.

	Jñāna	***Vijñāna***
1	Secular knowledge	Spiritual knowledge
2	Skills (*viṣaya naipuṇya*)	Understanding (*bodha*)
3	Knowledge describing objects	Knowledge that distinguishes an object from other objects
4	General knowledge (*sāmānya jñāna*)	Detailed, special or specific knowledge (*viśeṣa jñāna*)
5	Pure Science / Knowledge	Applied Science / Knowledge
6	Knowledge of diversity	Knowledge of unity in diversity
7	Knowledge of effects (*kārya jñāna*)	Knowledge of the cause of the effects (*kāraṇa jñāna*)

The various shades of meanings of the words *jñāna* and *vijñāna* from verse 42 to 48 are tabulated below:

	Jñāna	***Vijñāna***
42	The discrimination between the 'seer' and 'seen' (*dṛṣṭā-dṛśya viveka*)	Realising the Truth free from the 'seen' (*dṛśya śūnyatā*)
43	Knowledge of the Experiencer and the experienced (*kṣetra-kṣetrajña viveka*)	The realisation of the identity of experience (*aikya jñānam*) and the Supreme Self
44	Intellectual understanding of the Truth born from scriptural studies (*parokṣa śāstrajaṁ jñānam*)	Self-realisation (*ātmadarśanam*)
45	Understanding of 'thou' in the statement 'That thou art' (*tvam artha jñānam*)	Understanding of 'That' in the statement 'That thou art' (*tat artha jñānam*). *Jñāna-vijñāna* is to realise their essential oneness (*padayor-aikya jñānam*)
46	*Ajñānam* is to perceive the not-Self as the Self (*anyathā jñānam*), *Jñānam* is discrimination between the Self and not-Self (*ātmā-anātmā viveka*)	*Vijñānam* is to perceive that the Self pervades the world

47	The thought 'I am the infinite Truth' arising from right understanding (*brahmākāra vṛtti*)	The Realisation of the Truth free from all thoughts (*jñāna mātra*)
48	That which removes ignorance (*ajñāna dvamśakam*)	That which is of the nature of both knowledge and ignorance (*ubhayātmakam*)

42. In the deep-sleep state, each of us experiences the absence of the world. This homogenous, non-dual state is indeed Bliss. *Samādhi* is to attain this in the waking state. Realisation is to know that this objectless state is my essential nature and *sahaja samādhi* is to remain in this state even whilst perceiving the apparent duality.

43. The body is referred to as *kṣetra,* as it is a counter of experiences, good and bad (*bhogāyatanam*), a means by which we can perform good actions (*ḍharmāyatanam*), and a place wherein the individual resides (*nivāsa sthāna*). In a wider sense, *kṣetra* is a field of experience, that is, the entire world, including our body.

Vidura Neeti says, "He is indeed a wise man who realises the Lord that resides in this house (body) of nine doors (eyes, ears, nostrils, mouth, anus and genitals), the three pillars (*vāta, pitta, kapha*) and the five witnesses (the sense organs of perception).

Nava dvāraṁ idaṁ veṣma tribhagam pañcasākṣikam
Kṣetrajñā adhiṣṭhite vidvān yo veda sa paraḥ kaviḥ

The *Geeta* too says that the body is the experienced and the individual is the experiencer. However, the individual is in essence, the Supreme Self alone. [illegible]alisation is to know the identity of the individual [illegible]upreme Self.

[illegible]achings of the *Guru* and the study of the [illegible]ures result in intellectual conviction of [illegible]istence of Truth and ascertaining its [illegible]re. This gets transformed into Realisation [illegible]en one knows that the Self associated [illegible]with the individual body-mind equipment, and the Truth with its total conditionings, are in essence, one. In the first stage, we experience the joy of subtle thoughts and suffer the burning longing for Realisation. With Self-realisation, is experienced, unconditioned Bliss. Chaitanya Mahaprabhu cried in longing for the Lord and danced in Bliss on attaining Him.

45. Spiritual enquiry may start with the question, "Who am I?" or "Who is God?" In either case,

one arrives at the identity of both. This is Realisation.

46. The spiritually ignorant is convinced, 'I am the body'. The enquiring mind feels, 'I am the body and something else too—the individual dwelling in the body'. With discrimination, arises Self-realisation that "I am the ever-existing infinite Truth."

Deho'hamityeva jaḍasya buddhiḥ
Dehe ca jīve viduṣastvahaṁ dhīḥ
Viveka vijñānavato mahātmā
Brahmāhamityeva mati sadātmani—Viv[illegible]

47. The method of invariable concom[illegible] already explained in Verse 4. T[illegible] again used for the right understand[illegible] Truth. All effects must have an ultima[illegible] Existence or the Truth is the ultimate ca[illegible] everything. The ultimate Cause pervades the effect. In fact, it is this Cause alone that appears as the effect. However, in this Cause, there are no effects. In Existence or the Truth, there is total absence of all objects. The implications of this understanding gives rise to the thoughts 'I as the Supreme Consciousness am the ultimate Cause of this world, the infinite Truth or Existence'. On the cessation of this thought (*brahmākāra vṛtti*) there remains the pure

Existence-Consciousness (*Brahma*) alone—One without a second.

48. Knowledge dispels ignorance (*vidyā-avidyā nihantyeva*) just as light dispels darkness (*tejas-timira saṁghavat*). Ignorance of the Self manifests as the thoughts of finitude such as 'I am the body', 'I am fininte', 'I am the doer' etc. The knowledge 'I am infinite' destroys this wrong notion.

Actually the Self can never be unknown to us. I am and I know that I am. Yet I do not know who exactly I am. There exists therefore, both knowledge and ignorance regarding oneself (*bhāne api abhānam*).

The Self is of the nature of pure Consciousness (Knowledge). Being beyond the mind and senses, It is never known as an object (ignorance). Hence the Self is said to be both Knowledge and ignorance. Realisation is to abide in the infinite ever-existing Self.

* * *

We are all interested in having an 'out of the world' experience. Let us analyse our experiences to help us go beyond them.

भोक्ता सत्त्वगुणः शुद्धो भोगानां साधनं रजः ।
भोग्यं तमोगुणं प्राहुरात्मा चैषां प्रकाशकः ॥ ४९ ॥

bhoktā sattvaguṇaḥ śuddho bhogānāṁ sādhanaṁ rajaḥ |
bhogyaṁ tamoguṇaṁ prāhur-ātmā caiṣāṁ
prakāśakaḥ || 49||

49. भोक्ता = The enjoyer; शुद्धः = is the pure; सत्त्व-गुणः = *sattva guṇa*; साधनम् = (and) the instrument; भोगानाम् = of enjoyment; रजः = (is) *rajo guṇa*; प्राहुः = (the wise) say; भोग्यम् = object of enjoyment; तमोगुणम् = *tamo guṇa*; च = and; आत्मा = the Self; प्रकाशकः = (is the) illuminator; एषाम् = of these.

49. The enjoyer is pure sattva guṇa and the instrument of enjoyment is rajo guṇa. The wise say that the object of enjoyment is tamo guṇa and the Self is the illuminator of these.

The cause pervades the effects. The three inherent qualities (*sattva, rajas* and *tamas*) of *prakṛti*—the infinite power of the Lord, pervade the entire creation, which is made up of the five elements. *Sattva* is characterised by purity, knowledge and peace (*tatra sattvam nirmalatvāt prakāśakam anāmayam*). *Rajas* is activating and agitating, whereas *tamas* creates inertia and ignorance. The *tāmasic* aspects of these five elements form the gross world of objects, the *rājasic* aspects form the sense organs of action and the vital airs, and the *sāttvik* aspects, the sense organs of perception and the mind. In every experience, the objects (*tamas*) are experienced by the mind (*sattva*) through the senses which are powered by the vital airs (*rajas*).

Explained differently, the knower (*pramātā*) or the individual (*jīva*) is *sāttvik,* the instruments of knowledge (*pramāṇa*) or the senses or mind are *rājasic* and the known objects (*prameya*) or the world is *tāmasic.*

The world is experienced as thought modifications (*vartanāt vṛttiḥ*). The three qualities are seen in every thought modification. The form of the object (*viṣaya ākāra*) is *tāmasic,* the ego illumined by the reflection of Consciousness, the individual (*jīva*) is *sāttvik,* and the resultant modification (*vartanam*) that takes place when the individual and the world come together is the *rājasic* aspect of the thought.

The *Geeta* says, "Knowing that all experiences are a play of these qualities, the wise man remains unaffected by them" (*guṇā guṇeṣu vartante iti matvā na sajjate*). It further declares, "One who knows the Supreme Self beyond the three qualities, attains Me" (*guṇebhyaśca paraṁ vetti madbhāvaṁ so'dhigacchati*).

* * *

Verses 3 to 15 explained how our daily routine (*dina caryā*) can become *dhārmic* and a means to meditate on the Supreme. In the next four verses, each stage of our life (*jīvan caryā*) is similarly dealt with.

ब्रह्माध्ययनसंयुक्तो ब्रह्मचर्यरतः सदा ।
सर्वं ब्रह्मेति यो वेद ब्रह्मचारी स उच्यते ॥ ५० ॥

गृहस्थो गुणमध्यस्थः शरीरं गृहमुच्यते ।
गुणाः कुर्वन्ति कर्माणि नाहं कर्तेति बुद्धिमान् ॥ ५१ ॥

किमुग्रैश्च तपोभिश्च यस्य ज्ञानमयं तपः ।
हर्षामर्षविनिर्मुक्तो वानप्रस्थः स उच्यते ॥ ५२ ॥

देहाभ्यासो हि संन्यासो नैव काषायवाससा ।
नाऽहं देहोऽहमात्मेति निश्चयो न्यासलक्षणम् ॥ ५३ ॥

brahmādhyayana-saṁyukto brahmacarya-rataḥ sadā |
sarvaṁ brahmeti yo veda brahmacārī sa ucyate || 50||

gṛhastho guṇa-madhyasthaḥ śarīraṁ gṛhamucyate |
guṇāḥ kurvanti karmāṇi nāhaṁ karteti buddhimān || 51||

kimugraiśca tapobhiśca yasya jñānamayaṁ tapaḥ |
harṣāmarṣa-vinirmukto vānaprasthaḥ sa ucyate || 52||

dehābhyāso hi sannyāso naiva kāṣāya-vāsasā |
nā'haṁ deho'hamātmeti niścayo nyāsa-lakṣaṇam || 53||

50. ब्रह्म-अध्ययन-संयुक्तः = The one endowed with the study of the *Vedas*; ब्रह्मचर्य-रतः सदा = and revelling always in the vow of *brahmacarya*; यः = the one who;

वेद् = knows; सर्वम् = everything; ब्रह्म इति = as the Truth; सः = such a person; उच्यते = is called; ब्रह्मचारी = *brahmacārī.*

51. शरीरम् = The body; उच्यते = is called; गृहम् = the house; गृहस्थः = the *gṛhastha;* गुण-मध्यस्थः = seated admidst *guṇas.* बुद्धिमान् = The wise (house-holder knows); गुणाः = that the *guṇas;* कुर्वन्ति = do; कर्माणि = the actions; अहम् = I (am); न = not; कर्ता इति = the doer.

52. यस्य = For one; तपः = (whose) austerity; ज्ञान-मयम् = (is) of the nature of Knowledge; किम् = what is the purpose served; उग्रैः च तपोभिः च = by severe austerities. सः = He; हर्ष-अमर्ष-विनिर्मुक्तः = the one free of joy and anger; उच्यते = is called; वानप्रस्थः = *vānaprastha.*

53. निश्चयः = The firm determination; इति = thus; अहम् = I (am); न = not; देहः = the body; अहम् = I (am); आत्मा = the Self; न्यास-लक्षणम् = is the sign of renunciation; देह-अभ्यासः = this practice with respect to the body; हि = is verily; संन्यासः = *sannyāsa;* न एव = certainly not; काषाय-वाससा = the mere wearing of ochre robes.

50. The one endowed with the study of the Vedas and reveling always in the vow of brahmacarya, who knows everything as the Truth, is called a brahmacārī.

51. *The body is called the house; the gṛhastha is the one seated admidst the guṇas. The wise householder knows that it is the guṇas that do the actions and that he is not the doer.*

52. *For one whose austerity is of the nature of Knowledge, what is the purpose served by severe austerities? He who is free of joy and anger is called a vānaprastha.*

53. *The firm determination, "I am not the body but I am the Self," is the sign of renunciation. This practice with respect to the body is verily sannyāsa and is certainly not the mere wearing of ochre robes.*

Man passes through the four stages of life (*āśramas*), categorised as *brahmacarya* (student), *gṛhastha* (house-holder), *vānaprastha* (retired person) and *sannyāsa* (renunciate). *Āśrama* means a place of rest, a state free from burdens. *Dharma* guides us how to live a stress-free and wholesome life. We can excel at each stage, grow and outgrow each stage and prepare ourselves for the next stage. These stages are explained briefly below with respect to the age, the place where one dwells; the goals one pursues, the pursuits etc.

	Brahmacarya	***Gṛhastha***	***Vānaprastha***	***Sannyāsa***
Stage	Student	House-holder	Retired	Renunciate
Age	5 – 25 years	25 – 55 years	55 – 75 years	75 – 100 years
Place	*Gurukula* (residential school)	*Gṛha* (home)	*Vana* (home/forest) or *Āśrama* (hermitage)	*Aniketa* (wandering) or *Āśrama* (hermitage) or in solitude
Purush-artha (goals)	*Dharma*	*Dharma, Artha, Kāma*	*Dharma, Mokṣa*	*Mokṣa*
Pursuits	Study, Serve the Teacher, Spiritual practice	Earning, Support the rest, Spiritual practice	Spiritual practice, Service to society	Spiritual practice
Life characterised by	Study & discipline	Work & responsibility	Austerity	Sacrifice

A child till he/she went to the *Gurukula* (residential school) between 5 to 7 years did not fall into a formal stage of life (*āśrama*). At that age, the child does not have a sense of doership and lives on his whims and fancies and therefore has no formal duties towards himself or others.

The Vedantic significance and the realised man's experience of the four stage of life is now explained.

Brahmacārī: Living a life of self-control (*brahmacarya*), the seeker of Truth (*brahmacārī*) is immersed day and night in the study, reflection and contemplation of the Truth (*anena adhitena ahorātrān saṁdhadhāmi*). Such sincere study enables him to realise that all is the Truth alone (*sarvaṁ brahma iti veda*). He thereafter lives as the Truth (*brahmavat carati*) and revels in the Truth (*brahmaṇi carati*).

Gṛhastha: The body is the house (*gṛha*) in which the individual resides. The ordinary house-holder lives as the body and holds on to it and everything related to it with intense attachment. Some people do not even dispose fused bulbs! The realised man knows himself to be the indweller of the body of nine gates (*nava dvāre pure dehī*) totally free and independent. Maya Dānava created a beautiful palace of illusions for the Pandavas, who entertained themselves with its special features and characteristics. Duryodhana on the other hand, not knowing it's illusory nature was fooled many a time and suffered much indignity in the palace.

The ordinary man attributes the notion of doership on all that the body does. The realised man knows that he is neither the doer nor the initiator or instigator of any action (*naiva kurvan na kārayan*), but a mere sentient witness because of whom all actions take place. Pujya Gurudev Swami Chinmayananda sat through a three hour programme of poor quality with all attention! When asked about it, he said, "The spoken words produce sound waves which strike the tympanum creating vibrations which are conveyed to the brain, which analyses, understands and gives orders to the head to nod. In all this, why should I get bored!"

The ordinary house-holder does not use his intellect for enquiry into the nature of the Truth, but interacts and reacts unthinkingly (*man-mānī*). The wise *gṛhastha* uses his intellect (*buddhi-mān*) to enquire and know the Truth.

Vānaprastha: The life of a retired person was characterised by simple austere living. Austerity is to willingly endure physical discomfort or mental pin-pricks in order to achieve a higher goal. It is to refrain from indulgence so as to conserve one's energy, time and effort for achieving nobler goals. Austerities like fasting, silence etc. are taken up for controlling the mind and its desires and guiding it to higher pursuits. Some perform austerities like standing on one leg, physical deprivation, self-flagellation etc. Some do them only to achieve extra-ordinary powers (*siddhis*). However, even such severe penance by itself does not achieve freedom from desires, expectations, fears, anxieties, worry, anger, irritation etc. which seem to accost man especially in retired age.

"Shri Ramana Maharshi calls Self-enquiry which results in the destruction of ego great austerity"—*Upadeśa Sāra*.

aham apetakaṁ nija-vibhānaka.
mahad idaṁ tapo ramaṇa vāg iyam.

It is Self-realisation (*jñānamaya tapa*) that liberates us from the bondage of our mind and its expressions of pleasure (*harśa*), irritation (*amarśa*), fear (*bhaya*), agitation (*udvega*) etc. Hence one who performs such a penance is a true *vānaprastha*. Indeed the fulfillment of a retired life is in knowing the Self.

Sannyāsa: In the *Uddhava Geeta*, the Lord says, "Amongst the four stages of life, I am the fourth (*sannyāsa*)" (*āśrmāṇām ahaṁ turyo*) and "amongst the *dharmas*, I am renunciation" (*dharmāṇām asmi sannyāsaḥ*). *Sannyāsa* is thus described as the special glory (*vibhūti*) of the Lord. It is characterised by total reunununciation (*samyak nyāsa*).

In the other stages, the notion, 'I am a student, a house-holder or retired person' is emphasised so that man does his duty according to that stage. However, a *sannyāsi* should renounce even the thought, 'I am a renunciate'. This happens only when identification with the body and mind is renounced. Such renunciation leads to the Realisation of the immortal Self (*tyāgena eke amṛtatvam ānaṣuḥ*). Hence a Man of Realisation is a true renunciate and the fulfillment of *sannyāsa* is in Self-realisation and not just in donning the ochre robes symbolizing renunciation (*naiva kāṣāya-vāsasā*).

* * *

The second verse of this text reveals to us that the purpose of composing this text is Self-realisation. The last verse now tells us the result of the study, reflection and contemplation of the text.

सदाचारमिमं नित्यं येऽनुसन्दधते बुधाः ।
संसारसागराच्छीघ्रं मुच्यन्ते नात्र संशयः ॥ ५४ ॥

sadācāramimaṁ nityaṁ ye'nusandadhate budhāḥ |
saṁsāra-sāgarāc-chīghraṁ mucyante
nātra saṁśayaḥ || *54* ||

54. ये = Those; बुधाः = wise people; नित्यम् = (who) constantly; अनुसन्दधते = practise (study, reflect and

contemplate); इमम् = this; सदाचारम् = *Sadācāra*; मुच्यन्ते = get liberated; शीघ्रम् = quickly; संसार-सागरात् = from the ocean of transmigration; अत्र = in this regard; न = (there is) no; संशयः = doubt (whatsoever).

54. *Those wise people who constantly practise (study, reflect and contemplate) this* Sadācāra *get liberated quickly from the ocean of transmigration. In this regard, there is no doubt (whatsoever).*

We bathe regularly to wash off the grime collected from our daily travels through polluted roads and places. We are similarly advised to regularly study the words of the Scriptures to cleanse our mind of worldly *vāsanās* picked up during our daily transactions. Study of Vedantic texts like *Sadācāra* not only purifies the mind, but its reflection and contemplation helps us attain the very purpose of life, Self-realisation and Liberation from the cycle of birth and death.

This text takes us on a wonderful journey of various Vedantic contemplations explained in the language of our daily practices and good conduct (*sadācāra*). It guides us in reflection about many Vedantic concepts which aid meditation. These daily practices are meant to make us 'humane' and the meditation to help us know our 'divine' nature.

May we too, with our regular and diligent efforts, graced by God and blessed by our *Guru*, attain our divine Nature.

|| Om Tat Sat ||

|| śivārpaṇam astu ||